JB JOSSEY-BASS™
A Wiley Brand

T0300907

How to Harness the Power of Volunteers and Board Members in Fund Development

Scott C. Stevenson, Editor

WILEY

978-1-118-69210-3   ISBN

978-1-118-70414-1   ISBN (online)

How to Harness the Power of Volunteers, Board Members in Fund Development

Published by
Stevenson, Inc.

P.O. Box 4528 • Sioux City, Iowa • 51104
Phone 712.239.3010 • Fax 712.239.2166
www.stevensoninc.com

Chapter 1: Getting Started: Identify How Volunteers Can Help Fund Development Efforts 4

- Involvement Is Key to Giving
- Expand Opportunities for Involvement
- Give Volunteers Choices
- Eight Ways Volunteers Can Help in the Office
- Ease Volunteers Into Fund Development
- Focus on Enlisting, Grooming Volunteers
- Three Steps to Nurture Can-do Volunteers

Chapter 2: Volunteer Recruitment Strategies 7

- Introductory Letter Helps Surface Possible Volunteers
- Target Particular Groups With Involvement Opportunities
- Printed Piece Helps to Recruit New Ambassadors
- Engage More 'Up and Comers'
- Encourage Couples to Raise Funds for Your Cause
- Advice for Enlisting Volunteer Solicitors
- Show Clubs, Civic Groups How They Can Help
- Get Far-away Constituents Engaged in Your Cause

Chapter 3: Attracting and Engaging Board Members 11

- Ideal Board Member Qualities
- Be Up-front About Fundraising When Recruiting Board Members
- Groom Potential Board Members to Raise Funds Starting at Recruitment
- Ask Board Members to Sign Board Affirmation Agreement
- Ask Board Members to Commit to Fund Development Duties
- Invite Board Members to Introduce You and Your Cause
- Ask Every Board Member to Expose You
- Leverage the Powerful Reputations of Your Board Members
- Trade Large Events for Intimate Gatherings
- Turn Your Board Members Into Fundraisers
- Help Board Members Make Asks
- Engage Your Board in Selecting Their Funding Project
- Structure Purpose Into Board's Vice Chair Position

Chapter 4: Planning Procedures — Getting Involvement Early On 18

- Plug Volunteers Into Annual Planning Efforts
- You Gotta Know the Territory
- Tips for a Better Retreat
- Results-orientated Agenda Can Carry a Retreat
- Establish Objectives for Centers of Influence
- Make Volunteer Involvement a Part of Your Plans
- Get Your Board to Assume Responsibility for Annual Gifts

Chapter 5: Training and Education Procedures 21

- Volunteers Should Know the Cause They Represent
- Educate Volunteers, Staff With Fact-filled Flash Cards
- Help Volunteer Board Understand Solicitation Role
- Help Centers of Influence Open Doors on Your Organization's Behalf
- Help Centers of Influence Set Introductory Appointments
- Teach Volunteers How to Set the Appointment
- Prepare Board Members, Volunteers for Team Solicitations
- Prepare for Team Solicitation
- Train Volunteers to Ask for an Amount

- Involving Board Members in Fundraising Process
- Teach Board Members to Nurture Relationships
- Teach Board Members to Have Fun Soliciting Gifts
- Report Form Helps Solicitors Fulfill Expectations
- Create a Top-drawer Group of Major Gift Solicitors
- Equip Volunteer Callers With Solicitation Summary Reports
- Thank-you Calling Campaign Involves, Inspires and Educates Board Members

Chapter 6: Involvement Through Committees and Advisory Groups 29

- Active Committees Give Way to Increased Support
- Spell Out Committee Goals
- Business Advisory Council Helps Multiply Business Gifts
- Advisory Boards Welcome Involvement, Lead to Major Gifts
- Advisory Council Members Serve as Strong Advocates
- Feed Your Development Committee Fundraising Choices
- Nurture Your Development Committee Chair
- Train Chapters to Raise Funds on Your Behalf
- Give Your Auction Committee Some Direction
- Start a 'GOG' Club for Most Loyal Givers
- Form a Volunteer-driven Sponsorship Committee
- Cultivate Neighborhood Ambassadors

Chapter 7: Engaging Volunteers and Board Members in Annual Giving Efforts 34

- An Annual Fund Committee Might Be the Ticket for You
- Keep Your Annual Fund Committee's Platter Full
- Development Committee Needs Annual Goals, Too
- Ask Board Members to Secure $1,000-plus Donors
- Create Some Friendly Competition Among Board Members
- Energize Annual Giving Efforts by Engaging Younger Donors
- Establish a Cold Calls Committee
- Thorough Solicitation Script Helps Callers Ask for Gifts
- How to Identify, Attract Volunteer Callers
- Advice on Recruiting Volunteer Callers
- How to Attract 400-plus Volunteer Callers
- Telesolicitation That Includes Volunteer Callers
- Train Callers to Identify Clues to Giving Ability

Chapter 8: Volunteer Roles in Your Planned Giving Program 38

- Build an Active, Accomplished Planned Gifts Committee
- Planned Gift Committees Should Include the Creative
- Nurture a League of Planned Gift Ambassadors
- Engage Volunteers in Planned Gift Development
- Invite Planned Gift Donors to Make Board Testimonials
- Nurture Attorney Ambassadors
- Relationship With Professional Advisors Important
- Tips to Build a Strong Relationship With Professional Advisors

Chapter 9: **Engaging Fellow Employees in Fund Development** 41
- *Give Fellow Employees Easy Access to Fund Development*
- *Five Ways Employees Can Help With Fund Development*
- *Help Fellow Employees Cultivate Prospect Relationships*
- *Expand Your Donor Base*
- *Energize Fellow Employees*
- *Help Employees Cultivate Donors, Would-be Donors*
- *Educate and Train Fellow Employees*
- *Identify and Involve Employees About to Retire*

Chapter 10: **Turn to Retired Employees, Former Board Members for Help** 44
- *Involve Those From Your Past*
- *Stay Connected With Former Board Members*
- *Involve Former Chairpersons in Ongoing Idea Sessions*
- *Identify Retirees Who Will Lend Time, Expertise*
- *Connect With Your Nonprofit's Old Timers*

Chapter 11: **Engaging Volunteers and Board Members in Major Gifts Efforts** 46
- *Help Major Gifts Committee Establish a Routine*
- *Help Your Major Gifts Chair Know What's Expected*
- *Get Board Members Involved in Raising Major Gifts*
- *Endowment Committee Brings Focus*
- *Focus Centers of Influence On Million-dollar Prospects*
- *Create a Traveling Ambassador Corps to Assist in Cultivation*
- *Volunteer Recruitment Idea*
- *Link Traveling Ambassadors With Faraway Prospects*

Chapter 12: **Involving Volunteers and Board Members in Your Capital Campaign** 50
- *Unlock Your Board's Campaign Potential*
- *Focus Groups Prove to be Valuable Pre-campaign Tool*
- *Focus Group Questions Seek Community Input, Buy-in*
- *Focus Group Brings Forth Nontraditional Case Statement*
- *How to Identify and Recruit Your Next Major Campaign Chair*
- *Be Up Front About Chairperson's Expectations*
- *Don't Accept Just Anyone to Chair Your Campaign*
- *Appoint an Honorary Chair to Your Capital Campaign*
- *Establish and Share Steering Committee Duties*

Chapter 13: **Communicating With Board Members and Volunteers** 54
- *Assemble a Top-notch Toolkit to Boost Volunteer Involvement*
- *Handout Offers Ways to Help*
- *Offer Online Volunteer Sign-up*
- *Increase Board Productivity With a Dedicated Intranet*
- *Meet One-on-one With Board Members*
- *Expand Your Volunteer Base*
- *Keep Development Committee Members Up-to-date*
- *Breakfast With a Board Member*
- *Confirm Volunteer Assignments in Writing*
- *What Should You Report to Your Board and Volunteers?*

Chapter 14: **Management Issues** 59
- *Job Description Adds Substance to Centers of Influence Appointees*
- *How to Work With a High-powered Volunteer*
- *Monitor Key Contributions of Your Centers of Influence*
- *Volunteer Managers Assuming More Responsibility in Development Shops*
- *Deal With Deadbeat Volunteers*
- *Form Provides Helpful Way to Monitor Activity*

Chapter 15: **Showing Appreciation and Recognition to Volunteers and Board Members** 63
- *Recognize Fund Development Volunteers*
- *Feature Volunteer Leadership*
- *Give Volunteers Equal Billing*
- *Showcase Your Top Volunteer Solicitors*
- *Tout Campaign Leadership*
- *Unique Ways to Thank Your Campaign Steering Committee*

Chapter 16: **More Examples of How to Involve Volunteers, Board Members in Fund Development** 65
- *Eight Tips to Help Facilitate Successful Focus Groups*
- *Donor Testimonials Speak Volumes*
- *Do You Have a Guest Experts Program in Place*
- *Get a Letter-writing Campaign Underway*
- *When Money is Tight, Ask Donors for Time and Ideas*
- *Build Relationships by Hosting Dinner With Seven Strangers*
- *Donor Involvement Helps Raise Money With Little Cost*
- *Increase Major Giving With a Targeted Subcommittee*
- *Give Class Agents Clear Expectations*

How to Harness the Power of Volunteers, Board Members in Fund Development

GETTING STARTED: IDENTIFY HOW VOLUNTEERS CAN HELP FUND DEVELOPMENT EFFORTS

Sure, it does take time to identify, recruit, educate and support volunteers involved in fund development, but it's well worth it. Look at it as a long-term investment. Take the time up front and volunteers and board members will do more than you can imagine to build and expand your fund development success. It's an investment of time that will pay off in a big way, but it requires patience and ongoing attention to make it work.

Involvement Is Key to Giving

Involving donors in a cause is key to giving, especially in these economic times. Sounds simple, but too many nonprofits fail to do it.

Instead, the trend — especially in good economic times — seems to be to just ask for money with no strings attached, no donor involvement requested.

But times, they are a-changin'.

If you want current donors who may be pulling back to give generously again, involve them — in meaningful ways — in various aspects of your organization and its work. Ask them to speak to a class; ask for their input on your strategic plans.

To help donors and would-be donors maintain or regain ownership in your cause, give them opportunities to witness your good works first hand. Involvement is crucial when so many external forces are discouraging donors from giving.

Expand Opportunities for Involvement

How many specific involvement opportunities do you offer to both donors and would-be donors? Do you know? Have you ever identified each of them?

We all know that involvement leads to investment. That's why it's worth documenting every involvement opportunity that currently exists at your nonprofit. Make a list that includes categories and specific involvement opportunities within each category.

After doing that, meet with staff to review and discuss those existing involvement opportunities. Are there some with which you could be doing more to engage others? In addition, spend some time brainstorming involvement opportunities that aren't on the list. What additional entry points might be made available for donors and probable donors? Add them to your list. Talk about how to get the word out and enlist more people.

One word of caution, however, be sure that all involvement opportunities provide a meaningful experience. Otherwise, you will be doing more harm than good.

Create an internal document of all existing opportunities for involvement. Then add new opportunities.

George Mason University (Fairfax, VA) offers ways for alumni to get involved on its website. Check it out at: www.gmu.edu/alumni.

Piney Ridge Museum
Existing and New Involvement Opportunities

Fund Development Committee
- Sponsor an exhibit
- Secure exhibit sponsors
- Review prospect lists
New Ideas —
- Sign letters

Special Events Committee
- Plan, coordinate special events
- Sell tickets
- Set up, take down
New Ideas —
- Third-party events

Membership Committee
- Host prospective member events
- Coordinate a field trip
- Organize member recognition
New Ideas —
- Launch member chapters

Planned Gifts Committee
- Identify prospects
- Plan events
- Oversee memorials
- Recognize donors
New Ideas —
- Make attorney visits

Programming Committee
- Plan exhibits
- Catalogue artifacts
- Produce, manage historical documents
New Ideas —
- Develop outreach programs

Community & Public Relations Committee
- Organize receptions
- Provide tours
- Nominate, select awards recipients
- Offer newsletter contributions
New Ideas —
- Build, manage parade float

Youth Committee
- Become an officer
- Mentor someone
- Plan, coordinate educational offerings
New Ideas —
- Coordinate after school program

GETTING STARTED: IDENTIFY HOW VOLUNTEERS CAN HELP FUND DEVELOPMENT EFFORTS

Give Volunteers Choices

Many hands make light work. Right?

Well, your work load may not get any lighter, but if you work smart, volunteers can certainly help in fund development.

Whether you're just beginning to enlist volunteers or building on an existing program, the number of participating volunteers will grow if you offer them a menu of ways in which to get involved.

Develop a checklist of fund development actions and share it with board members, existing donors and those who have been active volunteers with your cause. Agree to one or more ways in which these individuals could assist in your advancement efforts.

Here's a sampling of actions from which volunteers can select:

☐ Sign appeal letters.
☐ Write personal notes of thanks.
☐ Make appointments for introductory calls.
☐ Establish a challenge gift.
☐ Make an annual and/or planned gift.
☐ Help cultivate major gift prospects.
☐ Review a proposal.
☐ Identify planned gift prospects.
☐ Cultivate agents of wealth on behalf of your organization.
☐ Act as hosts at fundraising events.
☐ Help rate/screen major gift prospects.
☐ Chair a membership campaign.
☐ Host a reception.
☐ Review/approve gift policies.
☐ Help with strategic planning.
☐ Serve on a search committee.
☐ Assist with tours.
☐ Chair your annual fund committee.

Any involvement in the fundraising process will help make these persons more gift-conscious and more willing to take on additional fundraising assignments.

Eight Ways Volunteers Can Help in the Office

Although you might think a volunteer who's adept at making face-to-face solicitation calls would be your top choice, there are other ways volunteers can assist in fund development and still provide considerable service. Here are several examples of ways volunteers can help with projects in your office:

1. **Records assistance** — filing, reviewing and updating files, data entry.
2. **Phone-related duties** — phone reception, making thank-you calls, setting appointments, conducting phone surveys, verifying information.
3. **Mail** — stuffing, sealing, packaging items, opening and/ or distributing mail.
4. **Writing** — signing letters, writing copy, producing handwritten notes.
5. **Design** — making posters or decorations for events, graphic design and layout.
6. **Managing** — supervising other office volunteers.
7. **Technological assistance** — Web-related, networking computers, installing software, e-mail related tasks.
8. **Number crunching** — producing reports, calculating numbers, making projections.

Ease Volunteers Into Fund Development

To involve more volunteers in fund development, go slowly. Help them overcome call reluctance by showing them they can do more than simply solicit gifts. As they become more comfortable and engaged, their enthusiasm for inviting support will increase. Here's an example of a conversation that follows this logic:

Staff member: "Susan, because of your belief in and longtime loyalty to our charity, I would like to invite you to join our Development Committee."

Volunteer: "Oh, I wouldn't be good at that. I'm not much for asking for money."

Staff member: "There is so much more to our work than simply asking for gift support. And as far as calls go, I'd only ask you to accompany me on some calls to thank donors for their generosity. Any soliciting of gifts could come at some later point, and only if you choose to participate.

Focus On Enlisting, Grooming Volunteers

If you work for a nonprofit that consists of a one-person development shop, invest a portion of your time, as much as 50 percent, to enlist and nurture volunteers who can boost your fundraising efforts significantly.

Consider these recruitment and training efforts:

✓ **Set clear expectations for your board's development committee.** Prepare a committee job description. Meet regularly (outside of board meetings) with this group. Partner with them in identifying quantifiable objectives that they will be expected to meet throughout your fiscal year.

✓ **Start an auxiliary.** Pull together two or three individuals experienced at leading volunteers and get them to buy into what an auxiliary could accomplish for your nonprofit.

✓ **Form a special events committee.** Ask some experienced event planners to come up with one or more fundraisers for which they can take responsibility throughout the year — a golf classic, a fashion show or some other fundraiser that makes sense for your organization and the audience they intend to reach.

✓ **Hand pick a few dependable volunteers willing to assist with internal matters**: filing, data entry, mailings, phone reception and other duties that will free up your time to focus on more important matters.

✓ **Coordinate a community-wide, volunteer-driven campaign.** Enlist co-chairs and captains who will then enlist others to conduct a highly visible 30-day campaign to raise funds from local businesses and individuals.

✓ **Form a planned gifts advisory board.** Assemble a small group representing agents of wealth — attorneys, trust officers, current planned gift donors, accountants — who will meet regularly to plan development, promotion and oversight of a planned gifts program on your behalf.

✓ **Establish a business partners program.** Call on a group of existing business donors to involve more businesses in the work of your organization. Come up with benefits for businesses that sponsor programs, make cash and in-kind donations and more.

Three Steps to Nurture Can-do Volunteers

Volunteers are infinitely valuable assets for any nonprofit. When you are fortunate enough to have a strong volunteer corps, do all you can to help these willing volunteers achieve fund development success. For instance:

1. **Give volunteers enough to do.** Show them you have high expectations of them.

2. **Give volunteers a time frame within which to carry out their assignments.** They obviously need a deadline, but if their responsibilities involve more than simply making a call, break their tasks down into components with an accompanying time frame that spells out what should be completed and by when.

3. **Be sure their assignments are meaningful** and not simply busy work. Explain to them the important purpose their duties fulfill and how those tasks help move your organization toward reaching its goals.

Make Assignments Face-to-face

Rather than sending volunteers a list of prospects on whom to call, meet face-to-face to go over assigned calls. This makes you more effective at assigning calls and them more committed to making them.

How to Harness the Power of Volunteers, Board Members in Fund Development

VOLUNTEER RECRUITMENT STRATEGIES

It's one thing to cast a net with the hope that you'll pull in scores of volunteers. It's another to identify and nurture those individuals who possess the ability to make a noticeable difference in your fundraising efforts. The recruitment methods you use to attract and engage volunteers will depend on how you intend to utilize them in fund development activities.

Introductory Letter Helps Surface Possible Volunteers

Could you use more volunteers helping with fund development? You may find the help you seek through a simple invitation directed to names already on your mailing list.

While phone calls and particularly face-to-face visits are the most effective means of recruiting volunteers, a personalized letter with a bounce back might help to surface those who have any interest in assisting with some aspect of fund development.

Develop a simple letter (like the one shown here) to send to all or a portion of those on your mailing list. Once you have sent the letter and received responses back, follow up with phone calls and one-on-one meetings with those who expressed interest.

> Dear <Name>:
>
> This time I am not writing to ask for your financial support but rather your time.
>
> To better meet the needs of those we serve, we need to generate far more financial resources than we have in the past. And to do that, we need the volunteer assistance of individuals who care about what we do and what we hope to accomplish.
>
> Could you give one hour of your time? Would you be willing to serve on a committee or sign letters? What about joining me in making calls on those who have given in the past — to thank them for their generosity?
>
> Whatever you can do, whatever you feel comfortable in doing, will be gratefully appreciated.
>
> If we are to expand our programs and accelerate what we are able to accomplish, we need the volunteer help of people such as you.
>
> Please review the enclosed checklist of ways in which you can assist with our fund development efforts, then check those that interest you and return the form. Once we receive it, we will be in touch with you to answer questions and discuss next steps.
>
> Thank you in advance for giving positive consideration to this important request.
>
> Sincerely,

Target Particular Groups With Involvement Opportunities

Want to generate more and increased gifts? Work at increasing involvement among both donors and would-be donors. As you know, involvement leads to investment.

To improve the level of involvement, however, strive to offer opportunities matching the interests of particular groups. For example, the volunteer projects you suggest to former board members may be different than those you would offer young professionals or recent high school graduates.

Examples of segmentation may include:

- Alumni
- Baby boomers
- Specific professions
- Parents
- Women/men
- Businesses
- Singles
- New graduates
- Church groups
- Civic organizations
- Retired employees
- Senior citizens
- Former board members
- Young families
- Environmental activists
- Scout or 4-H groups
- Families of those you serve
- Community service opportunities

After identifying targeted groups, develop involvement opportunity menus aimed at their interests and/or skills. Then market those opportunities through one-on-one visits, direct mail, online, group presentations and more.

This is an example of an inquiry card that could be used to encourage former board members to renew their involvement with a nonprofit.

Elkhorn Council
on Sexual Assault & Domestic Violence

Involvement Opportunities for Former Board Members...

Name _____
Address _____
City/State/ZIP _____
Phone _____ E-mail _____

- ❑ Mentor a new board member
- ❑ Host a reception
- ❑ Conduct stewardship calls
- ❑ Screen prospect names
- ❑ Make business contacts
- ❑ Help identify awards recipients
- ❑ Help host appreciation banquet
- ❑ Conduct VIP tours
- ❑ Help make new introductions
- ❑ Other _____

Printed Piece Helps to Recruit New Ambassadors

Could you use more centers of influence — friends of your organization willing to help identify, cultivate and even solicit new prospects capable of making significant gifts? To expand your pool of these active ambassadors, show new recruits what existing centers of influence are doing to help your charity.

Develop a printed piece that summarizes some of what existing centers of influence have been accomplishing on your behalf. A summary sheet, such as the example shown here, will help new ambassadors visualize what they might do to help cultivate new relationships on behalf of your organization. Depending on where they live, their occupations, where they travel and more, there are any number of ways in which they can help connect your organization to others of means.

As a side note, this handout also serves as an additional way to recognize existing centers of influence, so be sure they receive a copy of it as well.

Centers of Influence: How They're Making a Difference for XYZ University

Centers of Influence	Susan and Mark Goettler
Affiliation	Susan is a Board Member
Cultivation Event	Reception/dinner at their Florida residence
Location	Naples, Florida
Audience	Goettlers' Friends, Alumni/Friends of XYZ University
Date	Feb. 11, 2010 Number Attending 30
Summary	The Goettlers hosted a social hour and dinner at their winter residence in Florida. In attendance were two corporate CEOs who had no prior connection with XYZ University. As a result, one of the CEOs now serves on our board and recently made a six-figure first-time gift. In addition, two others attending the event have since made generous planned gift provisions for XYZ University.
Center of Influence	Howard Logane
Affiliation	Howard is a 1955 graduate living in Palo Alto, CA
Cultivation Event	Dinner with XYZ President, Howard and a friend
Location	Palo Alto, CA
Audience	One friend of Howard's
Date	May 5, 2010 Number Attending 3
Summary	Serving as a long-time Center of Influence on behalf of XYZ University, Howard arranged a dinner with a wealthy friend of his and XYZ University President. As a result of that initial meeting, Howard's friend has taken a keen interest in the university and made planned gift provisions that will amount to a seven-figure gift.
Centers of Influence	John and Ada Hobbs
Affiliation	Long-time local friends of the university
Cultivation Event	Four dinners per year
Location	Country club
Audience	Four different groups of friends/associates quarterly
Date	Jan. 15, April 23, July 12, Sept. 8, 2010
Number Attending	Eight individuals at each of the four dinners
Summary	John and Ada graciously agree to host quarterly dinners at their country club. They develop a list of possible invitees and run the list by Advancement Office staff. As a result, we are able to cultivate new and existing relationships with 32 people each year. These quarterly dinners have proven to be an indispensable way of building friendships and generating significant gifts.

Engage More 'Up and Comers'

Reach out to young professionals who are financially capable — or on their way to being so — based on their positions or inherited wealth, and reap big benefits in future years.

To begin to involve this younger group in your nonprofit:

1. **Set up focus groups.** Invite young professionals to share their thoughts about your nonprofit. Listen to their perceptions to learn more about what matters to them.

2. **Establish a young professionals advisory council** to take on projects to assist your organization. Provide them with ideas or let them come up with projects on their own.

3. **Encourage them to form a steering committee** to recruit others willing to become involved. Continue to provide a meeting place and support their efforts.

In addition to helping your efforts, this growing group of young professionals will become a source of longtime support for your organization and its mission.

Encourage Couples to Raise Funds for Your Cause

Don't underestimate the impact that two people working together can have on your organization's fundraising efforts. Here are four examples of couples that raised thousands of dollars each year for nonprofits:

1. Barbara and Arnold Schreibman have sold Reed & Barton silver holiday bells and donated all the proceeds to the Cleveland Orchestra for more than 40 years. They did so first through their own store and now through other retail outlets in their area, with the help of the Cleveland Orchestra Women's Committee. In 2006, they raised $4,500 selling the bells for $20 each.

2. For three years now, Cora and Charlie Venishel have held a Christmas Open House to raise money for the Ronald McDonald House. Each visit to their Christmas-theme decorated home in Penfield, NY, where Cora Venishel is dressed as Mrs. Claus, brings in a $3 donation. The couple raised about $700 the first year, $1,200 the second year, and hoped to raise $2,000 over the next year.

3. Julie and Bob Newman, owners of Love of Dog Bakery in Laurel, MD, donate 5 percent of their proceeds to a different charity each month.

4. Hawaiians Florence Doi and husband Takeshi Terada collect cans and 5-cent refundable bottles to raise funds to purchase rice, small toiletry items, medicine, Bibles and reading glasses for Cambodian villagers. The items are distributed through their church. In 2007, they bought $2,000 worth of rice (20,000 pounds) and 300 pairs of reading glasses. The couple also holds weekly garage sales to sell items dropped off by neighbors, friends and people who have heard of the sales through word of mouth.

Recruit Volunteer Couples

■ Next time you need volunteers, consider enlisting couples rather than individuals. Joint volunteering among spouses or couples offers an opportunity to spend time together and have fun working toward a worthwhile goal.

Advice for Enlisting Volunteer Solicitors

Building a group of proficient volunteer solicitors doesn't happen overnight. Follow these key steps as you build a competent team of solicitors:

1. **Identification** — Look to those who have a loyal history of giving and are enthusiastic about the work of your organization. Narrow your list to those prospects whose level of giving matches the capability of those you intend to approach.

2. **Enlistment** — Approach each solicitor candidate with a clearly defined scope of expectations: "I'm asking you to serve a two-year term which will include quarterly meetings followed by assigned calls." Share a position description that provides an overview of expected tasks.

3. **Training and education** — Incorporate training into all meetings. Have a staff member or experienced volunteer accompany new recruits on initial calls to ease them into this important process. Regularly share information that will help callers become more knowledgeable and passionate about your organization's programs and services. Share real life examples to which they can refer when making calls.

4. **Meetings** — Whether the group meets monthly or quarterly, develop a routine that includes reviewing names of potential donors, discussing solicitation strategies and assigning calls to be completed prior to the next meeting.

5. **Support and recognition** — Let your volunteers know you are there to support and assist them whenever needed. Continually applaud their efforts and accomplishments, both large and small. Your praise will keep them energized.

Show Clubs, Civic Groups How They Can Help

Do you give presentations to area clubs and civic organizations? Although education and awareness are no doubt a big part of those engagements, be sure to show those groups what they can do to help your cause.

Here's a sampling of what you can do:

• Share a printed wish list of needs from which clubs can select and help to address.

• Invite them to coordinate their own fundraising event with proceeds going to your charity.

• Distribute brochures that encourage individual members to contribute to your cause.

• Ask clubs to sponsor or adopt a particular program as volunteers — one that fits their mission.

• Partner with a group to sell something and split proceeds: ornaments, calendars, cookbooks, etc.

• Invite the club's members to help staff one of your day-long events.

Get Far-away Constituents Engaged in Your Cause

If your organization's work is regional, statewide or beyond, it's important to offer supporters who live some distance away the opportunity to get involved and engaged in your cause, especially as it relates to raising funds. Although the nature of involvement opportunities will vary depending on your type of nonprofit, here are several examples of how far-away constituents can get involved in various aspects of fund development:

- Begin a chapter.
- Clip and send news of interest to the advancement office.
- Introduce your cause to local agents of wealth — attorneys, trust officers, accountants, etc.

- Enlist new members.
- Assist with outreach programs.
- Make publicity appearances on behalf of the organization.
- Identify area prospects.
- Transport visitors for a visit to the main campus or headquarters.
- Coordinate a special event.
- Organize a local phonathon.
- Make thank-you calls on area contributors.
- Provide mailing list names.
- Host a reception.
- Distribute literature.

How to Harness the Power of Volunteers, Board Members in Fund Development

ATTRACTING AND ENGAGING BOARD MEMBERS

The approach you take in attracting and engaging board members is different from that of volunteers. More should be expected of board members as you engage them in fund development. They should set a precedent for giving as well as getting. Theirs is a higher calling. Likewise, the ways in which you utilize board members in fund development should reflect that higher calling. If you expect board members to assume a role in every aspect of fund development, they will soon become disillusioned. Involve them wisely and they will become energized.

Ideal Board Member Qualities

What qualities do you seek when considering new board members, especially those who can help strengthen your major gifts efforts? While there may be exceptions, here are some key characteristics to consider as you prioritize board candidates:

- Affluent
- Influential
- Connections to wealth
- Existing ties to your organization
- Belief in your mission
- Giving history to your nonprofit
- Ability to attend meetings

- Track record on other boards
- Ability to get things done
- Brings key talents to your board
- Willingness to be involved in fund development
- Respected by others
- Ability to enlist and motivate
- Follows through on projects
- Compatible with other board members and CEO
- Meets organization's gender, minority or other goals
- Ability to separate policy from management issues

Be Up-front About Fundraising When Recruiting Board Members

If you want a board that plays an active role in fundraising, you must be up-front about your organization's expectations with regard to fundraising during the board recruitment process, says Jean Block, president, Jean Block Consulting, Inc. (Albuquerque, NM) and author of "Fast Fundraising Facts for Fame and Fortune".

"It's not fair not to be honest up-front," Block says. "If you blur your expectations about fundraising, assuming that when it comes to making the ask they'll be on board about it, they won't. And some will even dig their heels in."

Board members should also be expected to advocate on the organization's behalf to people in their respective circles and make an annual contribution themselves, she says.

The fundraising expert shares eight ways to involve board members in fundraising:

1. **Secure grants from foundations and corporations.** Ask board members to research their own company's giving programs as well as other companies' giving programs. They can also provide testimonials and sign cover letters.

2. **Start a giving club.** Ask board members to set one up, name it, make the lead gift and recruit others to join.

3. **Assist with annual and direct mail campaigns.** Ask board members to provide testimonials for your fundraising letters, write personal appeal letters to names in their contact list, make thank-you calls on donors, make fundraising calls on donors and prospects, host an event at their home or office, or underwrite the campaign's cost.

4. **Get involved in your major gifts campaign.** Encourage board members to be aware of what's going on in the community, share what they learn about prospective major donors, assist in awareness, outreach, underwriting, sponsorships and in-kind gifts.

5. **Participate in special events.** Ask board members to plan, organize or serve on special events committees and/or sell tickets and solicit auction items.

6. **Make a personal planned gift.** Ask board members to help you with planned giving efforts by serving on a planned giving committee and soliciting planned gifts.

7. **Become an advocate.** Ask board members to contact lawmakers, testify and advocate on behalf of your organization's mission.

8. **Develop a social enterprise.** Encourage board members to lead your organization in developing an earned income venture (www.socialenterpriseventures.com).

Source: Jean Block, President, Jean Block Consulting, Inc., Albuquerque, NM. Phone (505) 899-1520. E-mail: jean@jblockinc.com

Groom Potential Board Members to Raise Funds Starting at Recruitment

Providing potential board members with clear expectations about fundraising when you are recruiting them is crucial to developing a board that is comfortable with and successful at fundraising, says Jean Block, author of "The ABC's of Building Better Boards" and principal of Jean Block Consulting, Inc. (Albuquerque, NM).

"If board members are not recruited and told expressly that fundraising is a part of their key responsibilities, why are we surprised when they balk at it?" the consultant says. "Too many nonprofits are so desperate for board members that they mumble about expectations for time, talent and treasure, they aren't specific about expectations, and then just hope the new board member will eventually get it."

Instead of using this bait and switch approach which ultimately leads to feelings of resentment by board members as they come to understand expectations for fundraising, Block says nominating committees must be honest, open and clear about their expectations for board members in the recruitment phase.

To present fundraising in a way that will get buy-in from the board, she advises:

- Emphasize the importance of the mission and the purpose of the organization.
- Present the realities of the organization's fiscal position.
- Discuss plainly, and up front, that fundraising is a key responsibility of each board member. "If the prospective board member isn't willing or able to fundraise, offer him or her another avenue to support the organization," she says.
- Lead by example. "How can an organization write grants, ask for donations, etc., if their own board has not set the example?" she says. "It just isn't ethical."

To ensure board members follow through with fundraising responsibilities, Block advises using an annual commitment letter, such as the one shown below, that specifically asks for a written commitment of the person's time, talent and treasure. In addition, consider offering a specific list of ways the board members can raise funds, such as the list Block shares at left.

"I also use a Board Give and Get Form to ensure accountability. If the Commitment Letter and Give and Get Form are not returned, then the board president meets with the board member to discuss other ways to support the organization's mission," she says, adding, "You need to sometimes start with baby steps, recognize and reward accomplishments and celebrate even small successes."

Source: Jean Block, Principal, Jean Block Consulting, Inc. & Social Enterprise Ventures LLC, Albuquerque, NM. Phone (505) 899-1520. E-mail: jean@jblockinc.com

Content not available in this edition

Ask Board Members to Sign Board Affirmation Agreement

At the Arts & Business Council of Greater Phoenix (Phoenix, AZ), board members are asked to sign an agreement that affirms their commitment to its mission, to their legal and fiduciary responsibilities, and to the council's success.

In addition to ensuring that board members know what is expected of them, the board affirmation agreement allows the organization to release board members who are not living up to their responsibilities, says Debra Paine, executive director.

One of their board members' fiduciary responsibilities is to either give or solicit at least $2,500 a year. If, for example, a board member did not fulfill this responsibility, says Paine, the board development chair would call the board member and remind him or her.

If the board member did not fulfill the responsibility after another month, the board chair would call again and let the person off the hook by letting them off the board.

"The board chair might say to the board member, for example," says Paine, "'We understand the financial times and that you've been unable to live up to your commitment. Maybe there will be a better time in the future when you can serve on the board. We're going to release you from your commitment.'"

Source: Debra M. Paine, Executive Director, Arts & Business Council of Greater Phoenix, Phoenix, AZ. Phone (602) 234-4711. E-mail: dpaine@artsbusinessphoenix.org

This board affirmation agreement clarifies the expectations of board members at the Arts & Business Council of Greater Phoenix (Phoenix, AZ).

Content not available in this edition

Ask Board Members to Commit to Fund Development Duties

If you fail to communicate expectations of board members to those board members, don't be surprised when they fail to meet those expectations.

To get board members to commit to helping your fundraising efforts, offer them a choice of three or four fund development options from which they can select. Then get them to commit to those choices.

At the start of a fiscal year or whenever a new board member signs on, share a fund development menu such as the example shown here. Explain what each involvement opportunity involves and then ask the board members to sign a commitment to follow through on whatever they chose.

As you prepare your menu of choices, you will need to decide what matters most: soliciting annual fund gifts, taking a leadership role in planning a special event, helping to identify and cultivate major and planned gifts, etc.

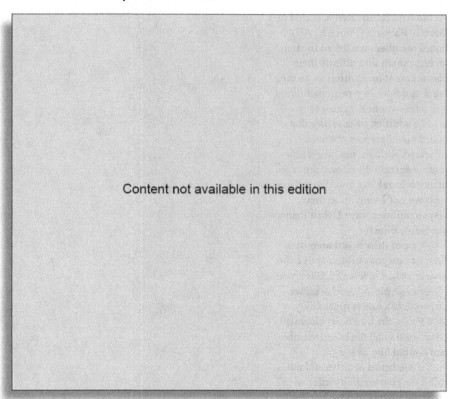

Content not available in this edition

Invite Board Members to Introduce You and Your Cause

Do you have a method to encourage board members to introduce you and your organization to individuals, businesses and foundations?

If your board is made up of movers and shakers, they should be in positions to help introduce your organization and assist in prospect cultivation. And for those board members who shudder at the thought of asking people for money, you can assure them that their primary role is simply to help make introductions and cultivate friendships. You or another advancement official can be prepared to make any asks.

Formalize your procedure for involving board members in this friend-making process by developing a form similar to the example shown. At a scheduled board meeting, ask board members to complete it and return it to you within a specified number of days. Then be prepared to begin following up with each board member immediately. (It's important to act while the assignment is still fresh in their minds.)

When you distribute the form, be sure to include your last honor roll of contributors so board members will be sure not to include names of those who are presently contributing to your organization. Better yet, also include a list of nondonors who would be likely prospect candidates.

Content not available in this edition

Ask Every Board Member to Expose You

To make new contacts with persons of wealth, be proactive in asking board members to include you in get-togethers with their friends and associates. Your simple presence could open doors leading to further meetings.

Extend an invitation for board members to think how they might include you as a friend in group get-togethers. Share some examples of how that might occur:

- Joining them as a guest at some other nonprofit's fundraiser.

- Accompanying them to a chamber of commerce event.
- Inviting you to join a foursome in a round of golf.
- Inclusion on their guest list for private dinner parties and receptions.
- Accompanying them to civic club meetings.
- Introductions to their company's top decision makers.

In addition, encourage board members to ask their spouses to include you in group gatherings if and when appropriate.

Leverage the Powerful Reputations of Your Board Members

Board members articulate strategic direction, provide organizational continuity and often supply their share of elbow grease to a nonprofit's mission. But beyond the services they provide, their reputation in the local, regional or national community can be of great benefit as well.

Larry Stybel understands how boards operate inside and out. He is co-founder and vice president of Board Options, Inc. (Boston, MA) — a nationally recognized company specializing in helping boards be effective problem-solving units through the application of practical behavioral science — and executive in residence at the Sawyer School of Business at Suffolk University (Boston, MA).

Here, Stybel shares his expertise in the art of leveraging the reputation of prestigious board members:

What is the central rationale behind showcasing well-known board members?

"Donors, when they were children, were told by their mothers that they would be known by the company they keep. This is what board members do for nonprofits. If you are an upcoming nonprofit that does not have top-flight status, one way to create reputation and cache is through your board members. In branded institutions like MIT or Princeton, the institution gives luster to the board member. But in smaller organizations, the opposite is true: board members lend their credibility to the nonprofit."

So in attracting donors and other prospective board members...

"Prestigious board members function like the anchor store of a shopping center, the place that all the other shops cluster around. If a brand-name person is on your board, other people will want to be associated with that individual, and, by extension, your organization and its mission."

Are there any challenges to having well-known board members?

"If you are not a prestigious institution, there is a limit to how

many brand-name people you can afford to have on your board. Two is great; six might not be so great. One of the disadvantages of bright star board members is that they often have only limited time to put into your organization. They will not typically be the 'shirtsleeves' board members who dig in and really get things done. Bright stars are important, but they are prone to fighting with each other, and too many can be counterproductive."

> "If a brand-name person is on your board, other people will want to be associated with that individual, and, by extension, your organization and its mission."

What should organizations know about using the name of a bright star board member?

"That it should always be done with the knowledge and agreement of the board member. That individual is lending his or her name and stature to your organization, and you don't want to abuse that privilege. A bright star should never find out you used his name after the fact. And also be aware that if he is a CEO or president, his business will often want to clear the use of the name beforehand as well."

Is there anything a shirtsleeves-heavy board should do or not do in looking for bright star members?

"One tip is to make board participation a finite commitment. Prestigious individuals don't want to be trapped on the board of a smaller nonprofit forever, even if they believe in its mission. Setting a term limit of two or three years spares them the awkwardness of resigning and makes them more likely to agree to the initial commitment."

Source: Larry Stybel, Co-Founder and Vice President, Board Options, Inc., Boston, MA. Phone (617) 594-7627.
E-mail: Lstybel@boardoptions.com

Trade Large Events for Intimate Gatherings

The annual fundraiser luncheon was an important donor acquisition vehicle, but expensive, says Michele Berard, director of funds development at Butler Hospital (Providence, RI). The event collected over $130,000 but netted only around $10,000.

So when corporate sponsorship fell in 2008, staff decided to drop the luncheon in favor of smaller cultivation events. The shift in strategy was potentially risky but paid off handsomely, with $1.2 million raised the next year.

Several factors led to the breakthrough, says Berard. The more individualized format played a role, as did a shift from general operating expenses to an endowed research fund. But leveraging the connections of board members was the key development.

"We asked them to hold gatherings in their homes and invite people they knew could help the hospital with major donations," she explains. "Some were hesitant, but we told them that all they had to provide was their friends — the development office would do the rest."

Accordingly, staff assembled packets of prospective donor information, ensured that doctors and administrators attended meetings to answer questions and concerns, and even produced a 12-minute video featuring hospital research projects.

But perhaps the most labor-intensive is the follow-up work staff does with contacts. No direct solicitation is made at the events, says Berard. Instead, the video presentation ends with a general appeal, and not until later are contacts called to discuss specific commitments.

Seven cultivation events have been held since the summer of 2009, resulting in gifts ranging from $1,000 to $20,000, with one outstanding contribution of $100,000. And significantly, the $1 million-plus already raised has come from just 70 gifts.

Source: Michele Berard, Director of Funds Development, Butler Hospital, Providence, RI. Phone (401) 455-6581. E-mail: mrberard@butler.org

Feed Your Board Members, Don't Eat Them

Board members are like chickens, says Michele Berard, director of funds development at Butler Hospital (Providence, RI). "You can eat your chickens to get the nourishment you need," Berard says, "but a much more sustainable approach is to give your chickens what they need to lay eggs for you."

The thrust of the analogy is clear: board giving is important, but board getting is crucial. To move beyond a single-minded focus on board members' treasure, Berard suggests refining the definition of board fundraising duties.

"Opening your home to others, putting staff in touch with friends, inviting acquaintances to events — it all counts as getting" she says. "When people hear they don't have to actually ask for money, they breathe a big sigh of relief. And then they are much more willing to help."

Turn Your Board Members Into Fundraisers

Want to get your board members more involved in fundraising? Just ask.

Staff with the nonprofit Advocates for Youth (Washington, DC) ask board members to fill out and sign a commitment form that outlines various ways they can help raise money for the organization throughout the year.

"It's important to recognize that some board members won't be comfortable fundraising, no matter what you do," says Elizabeth H. Merck, manager of individual giving. "The key is to figure out a way that they can get involved in fundraising that doesn't intimidate them."

The form provides about 20 options for board members to choose from, including:

❑ Serving on the fundraising committee.
❑ Making phone calls to thank donors for their gifts.
❑ Writing personal notes on fundraising appeal letters.
❑ Pledging to shop online using GiveBackAmerica.org.
❑ Sending informational packets to five people by mail and asking them to make a gift.
❑ Providing the names of five individuals to add to the mailing list.
❑ Providing an introduction to at least one major donor prospect.
❑ Hosting an event.
❑ Pledging to search the Web using GoodSearch.

Merck follows up with board members throughout the year to make sure they're fulfilling their commitments.

Source: Elizabeth H. Merck, Manager of Individual Giving, Advocates for Youth, Washington, DC. Phone (202) 419-3420 ext. 24. E-mail: liz@advocatesforyouth.org

Board Involvement Tip

■ To get your board more involved in fund development, invite individual board members to accompany you on stewardship calls to thank donors who recently made gifts at higher levels. Board members will be energized by the experience and become more inclined to accompany you on future solicitation calls. Bonus: donors will appreciate having a board member along to say thanks.

Help Board Members Make Asks

When it comes to asking others for gifts, do your board members drag their feet?

Christina Thrun, development and marketing director, Big Brothers Big Sisters of Northwestern Wisconsin (Eau Claire, WI), shares a method her organization uses to get board members over their hesitation and engaged in seeking gifts: The Big Magic Breakfast, which has helped board members raise nearly $250,000 since 2004.

The event is based on the Raising More Money or Benevon Model of fundraising, which trains and coaches nonprofit organizations to implement a mission-based system for raising sustainable funding from individual donors.

For the breakfast, board members serve as table captains and fill a table of seven by inviting friends and colleagues. Staff provides them with tools and information on how to ask guests to participate, which makes it easier for them. No mass invitations are sent out for the event, which is designed to generate multiple-year gifts.

The breakfast runs 7:30 to 8:30 a.m. and includes a program that is about 35 minutes long with speakers such as the organization's CEO and board president, a volunteer/mentor and someone involved in the school system who can speak to the organization's impact on students.

At the end of the program, table captains pass out pledge cards and the board president asks people to make a gift.

Thrun says, "This event is a bit more of a high-pressure ask, but it's not a direct ask. By doing this event, our board members don't have to visit with people one on one and ask them to make a gift. Many of our board members really like this event and have chosen these events over the one-on-one approach."

She says the event has also been popular among donors and invited guests. "We've received a lot of great feedback from guests, who indicate how moving the event is. We've yet to have an event with completely dry eyes."

Source: Christina Thrun, Development and Marketing Director, Big Brothers Big Sisters Northwestern Wisconsin, Eau Claire, WI. Phone (715) 835-0161. E-mail: Christina.Thrun@bbbs.org

Engage Your Board in Selecting Their Funding Project

Want to raise the level of annual giving among your board members? Involve them in a process that allows them to select their own funding project.

Begin with your staff by identifying a list of potential projects the board might find appealing. Select only those projects whose price tag is high enough to stretch board giving. If, for example, you have 15 board members and it's your hope to raise the yearly average board gift to $1,500, select projects that can't get realized without a cumulative commitment of $22,500 or more.

Also, make it clear that the project they select will not be made possible unless the goal is fully reached by a particular date.

After developing a handful of funding projects, present them to your board's development committee to review and discuss. If this committee understands and owns what you are attempting to accomplish, they will be better equipped to sell the remaining board members when it comes time to select and approve a funding project.

Structure Purpose Into Board's Vice Chair Position

All too many organizations elect a vice chair without expecting him/her to do anything more than fill in when the chairperson is unable to attend a meeting.

But doing so is a big waste of talent and resources.

Why not assign special duties that allow your vice chair to accomplish some special fund development projects and prepare him/her for eventually assuming the chairperson's role?

Need some examples? Consider assigning your vice chairperson to:

1. Head up your development committee.
2. Lead the effort to focus on stewarding and expanding the number of annual $1,000-and-above donors.
3. Mobilize a campaign to raise funds for a special restricted-gift project.
4. Chair an event that reaches out to new donors.
5. Host a series of prospect rating and screening sessions throughout your community or region.
6. Oversee an annual awards program that selects recipients based on various achievement categories.

How to Harness the Power of Volunteers, Board Members in Fund Development.
Edited by Scott C. Stevenson.
© 2010 Stevenson, Inc. Published 2010 by Stevenson, Inc.

How to Harness the Power of Volunteers, Board Members in Fund Development

PLANNING PROCEDURES — GETTING INVOLVEMENT EARLY ON

If you build it, they will come? No.... if THEY build it, THEY will come. It's critical that volunteers and board members be involved in planning fund development activities. Engaging them early on will help to build their ownership in your programs. They will strive for success because they helped shape the plans and goals. Give them every opportunity to help plan and establish their own quantifiable objectives.

Plug Volunteers Into Annual Planning Efforts

Would you like volunteers to become more engaged in your fundraising efforts? Then work to involve them in planning your year and in shaping specific fundraising strategies.

Whether it is by participating in planning a retreat, being a part of a focus group or meeting with you individually, ask for volunteer input that will set the stage for continued involvement as the fundraising year progresses.

Volunteers can help plan by:
• Developing an annual giving theme.

• Reviewing and commenting on your yearly operational plan.
• Brainstorming new approaches for increasing overall gifts.
• Planning a yearly campaign kickoff event.
• Reviewing and commenting on specific fundraising programs (e.g., phonathon, community campaign, gift clubs and accompanying benefits, etc.).
• Brainstorming funding opportunities that might most appeal to the giving public.

You Gotta Know the Territory

Whether you're a field officer in Cincinnati with headquarters in Baltimore or you work out of your charity's home office but have been assigned fundraising responsibilities for the Upper Midwest, it's important to learn how to identify regional wealth when you're less familiar with the territory.

If you're fortunate enough to have a territory that stops at the city limit (as in the Cincinnati example), the job becomes somewhat easier than if your region covers a wide multi-state area. In either case, however, listed below are several avenues for pinpointing your territory's movers and shakers:

• Regularly review your organization's mailing list and files to identify those who have existing relationships with your cause. Those donors and persons with an existing link should begin as top prospects.
• Establish volunteer advisory groups based on geographic boundaries (e.g., neighborhood, county, community)

whose members serve as centers of influence, identifying, researching, cultivating and even soliciting individuals and businesses in their respective areas.
• Review newspapers, business and trade journals, identifying new prospects.
• Become a member of local Chambers of Commerce where appropriate and attend their functions when possible.
• Every time you make contact with someone, ask for referrals.
• Attend community events and become involved in one or more civic groups that provide the best contacts.
• Create outreach strategies that bring prospects to you: a get-to-know-us reception sponsored by a local business; appearances on television and radio that allow you to extend invitations and more.

Tips for a Better Retreat

Retreats are a great way to rejuvenate staff, board members or volunteers. To get the most out of your next retreat:

1. **Get everyone thinking about how to make the organization better.** Open your retreat with a thought-provoking question such as: "For our organization to be successful, we must be especially good at the following activities..." Then have everyone spend a few moments writing at least three answers to the question and then read their answers to the group. Get a consensus of the different ideas and write each on a flip chart or board so all can see. Now discuss how to achieve those activities or goals.

2. **Keep a reminder list.** Have a reminder list on a flip chart or board. Whenever a topic arises that would fit better at a later time on your agenda, jot that topic down on the reminder list. By doing so, you'll confirm your promise to return to that item.

3. **Ask two critical closing questions.** During the final hour or so of your retreat, ask participants what they learned at the retreat and what they intend to do with that new information when they get back. Have them write down what was important to them so they have a permanent record of what they learned.

Results-oriented Agenda Can Carry a Retreat

No matter what a retreat's purpose, its success starts with a strong agenda.

"A well-planned retreat will build a stronger team, resolve issues through brainstorming and consensus building and will end with strong action items and follow-up plan," says consultant KC Henry, principal, Transitions Unlimited (Chagrin Falls, OH). "The team will feel motivated and that their time was invested well."

To create a results-oriented agenda, Henry says the first step is to identify your organization's needs and determine your retreat's goal (e.g., build consensus on a specific issue, develop a plan for an upcoming capital campaign, create short-or long-term goals and team building).

Next, effectively communicate this goal with the facilitator so that together you can create a results-based agenda.

While agendas vary depending on goals, Henry says a typical agenda includes:

- **Introductions and a team-building activity.** The activity should make participants feel comfortable working together in a group setting.

- **Assessment reports** on the status of each issue to be discussed. Distribute these reports in advance.

- **A presentation** by an expert in your organization's field of interest.

- **Small group breakout sessions.** These sessions allow attendees to work with a variety of people and also to get up and move. Each group should be assigned its own facilitator who can encourage participation from every member.

- **Breaks and treats.** Henry recommends breaking at least once every two hours, and food and snacks are a must.

- **Consensus building.** This process is one of the most critical goals. Avoid majority votes in decision making. A facilitator should help find consensus, even if that means to agree to disagree.

- **Wrap up.** Develop action items. Include a timeline and indicate who is responsible for each item. "The outcomes of the retreat are what shows if the retreat was successful or effective," Henry says. "Leave plenty of time to create action items and an implementation plan to be sure there is good follow through."

Even with a carefully crafted agenda, remain flexible, Henry advises. "Sometimes certain agenda items can take longer than expected," she says. "Flexibility is important. Only put general, not specific, time frames on agenda items. If discussion gets bogged down on certain items and consensus is not forthcoming, get agreement to put that agenda item on hold to address later. The issue may need additional research or input from other sources to clarify direction."

Source: KC Henry, Consultant, Transitions Unlimited, Chagrin Falls, OH. Phone (440) 543-8306. E-mail: kchenry@transitionsunlimited.net. Website: www.transitionsunlimited.net

Establish Objectives for Centers of Influence

How many centers of influence — volunteers who have agreed to assist you in some capacity with fund development — do you have scattered throughout the community, region or nation working to assist your fundraising efforts?

These willing ambassadors can help significantly in identifying major or planned gift prospects, promoting your cause among friends, relatives and colleagues and much more.

Develop a list of quantifiable objectives to build the number of centers of influence working on behalf of your charity.

These examples will get you started:

- Identify and recruit two or more centers of influence for each county within your state.

- Instruct all existing centers of influence to recruit at least two more members of their communities to serve as centers of influence.

- Make no less than three face-to-face visits with each existing center of influence during the course of the fiscal year.

- Produce and distribute a centers of influence job description to no less than 50 ideal candidates throughout the year.

- Convince at least 50 percent of existing centers of influence to host a reception on behalf of your charity.

- Invite existing centers of influence to your facility for a day to train them and recognize their commitment.

- Generate 5 percent of this year's annual fund goal through center of influence solicitation calls.

Make Volunteer Involvement a Part of Your Plans

As you prepare an operational plan for your fiscal year, be sure to include a volunteer component. Volunteers can really allow you to accomplish more if you have put ample thought into planning for their involvement. And by delegating tasks to volunteers, you'll have more trained staff time available for other duties.

Pencil volunteers into your year plan for any number of tasks, including:
- Making solicitation calls.
- Reviewing, rating and screening prospect names.
- Making phone calls.
- Calling donors to say "thanks".
- Taking photos.
- Helping coordinate special events.
- Serving as centers of influence.
- Assisting with behind-the-scenes duties such as stuffing envelopes.
- Staffing informational booths at community events.

Your written operational plan — complete with goals, quantifiable objectives, action plans and a master calendar for the year of who does what and by when — may have various volunteer-related actions scattered throughout, or you may choose to have a separate section that focuses solely on volunteer plans.

A generic example of volunteer planning is shown at right:

2010/11 Operational Plan
Manilla School

Volunteer Involvement Objectives

Objective No. 1: To manage the Board Development Committee (six members) and support them in generating $4,000 in new annual fund gifts.

Objective No. 2: To coordinate, manage two phonathons (Fall and Spring) that include no less than 35 volunteer callers. (Phonathon goal: $18,500)

Objective No 3: To coordinate and manage the Golf Classic Planning Committee made up of no less than eight volunteers. (Golf Classic goal: $10,000)

Objective No. 4: To manage the work of Annual Awards Committee (five members).

Objective No. 5: To coordinate and manage the annual Community Campaign made up of no less than 40 volunteers who will seek gifts from throughout the community. (Community Campaign goal: $50,000)

Volunteer Programs Calendar

Month	Action	Responsible
June	Recruit phonathon co-chairs	Miller
July	Recruit phonathon callers (20-plus)	Miller
August	Recruit Community Campaign chair, leadership	Gray
September	Recruit Community Campaign volunteers	Gray
September	Board Meeting — meet w/Development Committee	Gray
September	Hold Fall Phonathon	Miller
October	Community Campaign Kickoff	Gray
January	Board Meeting — meet w/Development Committee	Gray
February	Recruit phonathon callers (20-plus)	Miller
February	Recruit Golf Classic chair, vice-chair	Fennel
March	Meet with Golf Classic chair, vice chair; recruit committee	Fennel
April	Hold Spring Phonathon	Miller
May	Board Meeting — meet w/Development Committee	Gray
May 15	Annual Golf Classic	Fennel

Get Your Board to Assume Responsibility for Annual Gifts

It's not uncommon for boards to think "it's the responsibility of staff to meet annual fund goals." That's wrong. Board members should feel some sense of ownership for meeting and exceeding annual gift goals.

Engage your board in annual giving by getting them to approve some portion of your annual giving goal. Depending on your board's size and level of past involvement, convince the board development committee to accept responsibility and seek full board approval for any of these yearly goals:

✓ To secure [X] number of gifts throughout the fiscal year within a defined gift range (e.g., $500 and above).

✓ To individually sell so many special event tickets each year (or purchase those they don't get sold).

✓ To individually contribute a minimum amount to the annual fund each year.

✓ To individually make a minimum number of solicitation calls on new prospects.

How to Harness the Power of Volunteers, Board Members in Fund Development

TRAINING AND EDUCATION PROCEDURES

Advancement professionals sometimes become disillusioned with the idea of involving volunteers in fund development, and often times that's because the volunteers didn't receive proper training and education to accomplish what was expected of them. Recruiting capable volunteers is only half of the job; it's equally important to train them and continue to nurture them as a vital part of your development team. And to keep them motivated, recognize that training and education can be provided in a variety of ways.

Volunteers Should Know the Cause They Represent

If you're counting on volunteers making calls on behalf of your organization — soliciting gifts, conducting a membership campaign or asking for donated items for your special event — it's reasonable to expect them to have a better understanding of your cause than the average citizen. The more they know about your organization and how it works, the more effective they will be when it comes to soliciting gifts.

Whether you give a brief quiz or address the topic as part of volunteer training, determine if volunteers know the answers to basic questions such as those listed at the right:

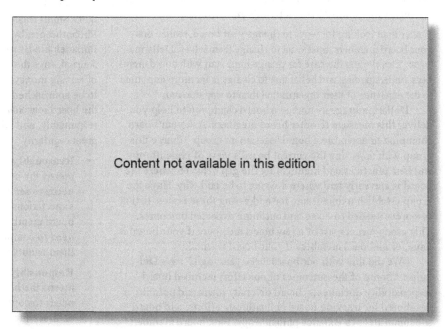

Content not available in this edition

Educate Volunteers, Staff With Fact-filled Flash Cards

Ongoing education for staff and volunteers needn't be complicated. In fact, it can be child's play.

Recalling childhood teaching methods, officials with the Iowa Council of Foundations (Des Moines, IA) developed a new training tool similar to flash cards.

According to Angela Dethlefs-Trettin, director, the need to provide education on asset development led the organization to create the first in a series of training cards aimed at assisting local governing body members in their familiarity with the practices and opportunities with their community foundations.

The cards, similar to flash cards used in grade school, are presented in a board game providing commonly asked questions as well as responses that help volunteers and staff become more comfortable about sharing community-based philanthropic information.

Introduced in October 2007, the first set of cards, "A Board Game for Endowment Building," offers 30 scenarios with answers plus 20 blank cards for local community foundations to develop their own commonly asked questions.

Community foundations statewide use the cards.

"The board game is really a game for the board to develop and use as they see fit for sharing and gaining information related to endowment building," says Dethlefs-Trettin.

She says the cards can be used in a number of creative ways, such as:

- To spur one-on-one conversation between current

governing board members and new members;

- In large group discussions at governing body or committee meetings and trainings;

The Iowa Council of Foundations (Des Moines, IA) uses flash cards to educate volunteers and staff about philanthropic issues.

The organization has produced a second series of the cards on leadership to provide insight into various aspects of leadership of local community foundations (e.g., issues related to best practices in governance, conflict of interest issues, governing body recruitment, etc.). Dethlefs-Trettin says additional topics may be added in the future.

Source: Angela Dethlefs-Trettin, Director, Iowa Council of Foundations, Des Moines, IA. Phone (515) 537-6956.
E-mail: info@IowaCouncilofFoundations.org

Help Volunteer Board Understand Solicitation Role

Major gifts success starts and ends with inside support. But what if your current volunteer-based board is not as clearly focused on raising major gifts as you would prefer?

Here, three fundraising experts share their insight on how to reshape your volunteer-based board into one more focused on fundraising:

Sondra Dellaripa, Vice President of Development, Eastern Connecticut Health Network (Hartford, CT):

Rather than looking for ways to change your board, realize that your board members must want to change themselves. Dellaripa says: "Developing the case for change must start with board members' understanding and belief that to change is far more important to the existence of their organization than to stay the same."

Dellaripa suggests finding a board champion to help you deliver this message to other board members. Ask your board champion to assemble a board assessment group. Charge this group with assessing the current board's view of philanthropy and best practices and highlighting the gap between where the board is currently and where it wants to be and why. Have the group establish a time frame for addressing these issues, listing resources needed to do so and outlining expected outcomes. This group can consist of a few board members if your board is large, or all board members if your board is small.

"We did this with our board three years ago," says Dellaripa. "Some of the outcomes of our effort included board responsibility documents, board diversity plans and policies, a dashboard for tracking board philanthropy efforts, and board subcommittees to enhance philanthropy. First board members' thoughts changed, and then their behaviors. Our board members are now more satisfied, and feel successful and proud of their efforts, knowing they did this for themselves."

Aaron Berger, Partner, Alexander Haas (Atlanta, GA):

Adding a half- or full-day to your board retreat to allow board members to look at their own roles, expectations, effectiveness and satisfaction is a great way to allow your individual board members to suggest specific goals for themselves. Berger says: "This way touchy topics like board giving, board member responsibilities, term limits, conflicts of interest, etc., can be discussed as peers in a constructive way."

Kayte Connelly, Chief Solutions Officer, Principled Solutions LLC (West Chester, PA):

According to Connelly, many times boards are stuck because their members do not understand their roles as chief policy makers.

"Policy dictates all money issues — spending money,

watching money, raising money," she says. "Executive directors may experience a setback because their board gets mired in muck and can't move on to the issues of money."

Connelly, named 2009 Small Business Philanthropist by the Philadelphia Business Journal, says the task of raising money needs to be approached by the board reasonably, responsibly, and with great regularity:

- **Reasonably** means the board needs to set clear expectations and board members need to commit to them annually.

- **Responsibly** means the board needs to conduct an assessment and provide training for areas where remedial actions are needed to support the board's work.

- **Regularly** means the board needs to use frequent accountability measures throughout the year, in the form of quarterly reports through committee actions, individual actions, etc. "These types of reports can propel the worst of boards forward in their goals," she says.

Training Tips For Volunteers

When turning to volunteers to set appointments with campaign prospects, caution against sharing too much information by phone. Their goal should be a face-to-face meeting, not an over the phone response.

Give volunteers a couple of responses they can use to emphasize the necessity of a sit-down meeting:

✓ "It's important to me, Bill, to meet face-to-face and bring you up to date on this campaign."

✓ "I would be doing both you and the college a disservice if we tried to address this topic over the phone. I really need a half hour of your time, Bill."

Sources: Aaron Berger, Partner, Alexander Haas, Atlanta, GA. Phone (404) 525-7575. E-mail: aaron.berger@fundraisingcounsel.com
Kayte Connelly, Chief Solutions Officer, Principled Solutions LLC, West Chester, PA. Phone (484) 769-2327.
E-mail: Kayte@bestprincipledsolutions.com
Sondra Dellaripa, Vice President, Development & Major Gifts Officer, Eastern Connecticut Health Network, CT Foundation & Philanthropy Consultant, Manchester, CT. Phone (860) 647-6877.
E-mail: sdellaripa@echn.org

Help Centers of Influence Open Doors on Your Organization's Behalf

Board members and volunteers may be more willing to assist your cause if you let them know how easy it is to help.

Take the topic of introducing your organization to new prospects, for example. Just imagine the multitude of colleagues and friends known by each of your board members. Of those many circles of contacts, how many presently contribute to your organization's work? Probably tons of potential there!

Now just imagine how much more willing and enthused board members would be about introducing you and your cause to their contacts if you showed them how easy it would be to do so.

By taking the time to develop one or two letters board members and other volunteers could use as a tool to make introductions, you can help these committed individuals visualize the ease of linking your organization with their friends and associates.

After developing an introductory letter that board members and other centers of influence can use as a template, follow these steps:

1. Share the sample letter(s) whenever the opportunity presents itself — at board meetings, during one-on-one meetings and so forth.

2. After the sample letter has been reviewed, ask the centers of influence to list a handful of individuals to whom they would be willing to send the letter. Explain that the letter would carry more weight if typed on their own business or personal letterhead.

3. Ask the board members and volunteers to give or send you a copy of the letters once they are sent.

4. As you receive letters, contact the sender to begin coordinating schedules to set up introductory visits.

5. Once an appointment is successfully scheduled, meet with your contact in advance to discuss the meeting's primary objective and your presentation format (who says what).

If even a handful of board members and others follow through on sending letters and setting up appointments with prospects, the effort will be worthwhile.

Craft one or two introductory letters, such as the example below, that board members and others can use as a template to set up visits with new prospects.

Williams & Company, Inc.
Frank W. Williams, Chairman

July 12, 2010

Dear Tom:

I'm going to get right to the point: I would like you to meet with me and Pam Hastings, Executive Director of the Council on Sexual Assault and Domestic Violence, at your convenience. We want to bring you up to speed on this organization and its work. I promise we'll limit our visit to no more than 45 minutes of your time.

You and I have known each other as friends for many years, Tom. And because I know how genuinely interested you are in the future of our community and the quality of life of our citizens, I want you to learn of this organization's value.

As I think you know, I serve on the board of directors for the Council on Sexual Assault and Domestic Violence. This organization, now in it's 12th year, works to assist both individuals and families — throughout a seven-county region — who are suffering as a result of sexual abuse and/or domestic violence.

I can't begin to tell you how much good this organization is accomplishing in assisting families in need, Tom. And believe me, our community and this region certainly have many families in need!

I'd really appreciate your willingness to learn about this important organization and its programs. Then you can decide whether it's worth your time to invest financially in its efforts, become involved in some capacity, or both. I will plan to give you a call sometime during the next two weeks to coordinate a time that will work for both you and Pam Hastings.

Thanks in advance, Tom, for your willingness to lend us a few minutes of your time.

Sincerely,

Frank Williams
Board Member
Council on Sexual Assault & Domestic Violence

Williams & Company • PO Box 9999 • Fair Oaks USA • Phone (999) 999-9999 • Fax (999) 999-9991

Help Centers of Influence Set Introductory Appointments

Most veteran development professionals will agree that making cold calls is an uphill battle. Setting an appointment can, in itself, be a nearly impossible task — unless you have the right person doing it for you.

Enlist the help of your organization's current friends and supporters, your centers of influence, to help gain entry into the homes and offices of new prospects, especially those capable of making generous annual gifts.

To help centers of influence help you, develop an introductory letter they can use as a template in developing letters of their own. The letter can be used by these willing volunteers as a first step in setting an appointment with new prospects, friends and associates of theirs who might be willing to contribute to your cause. Providing these volunteers with a sample introductory letter will take the guesswork away and show them how easy it is for them to help gain access to their friends and associates.

Encourage willing centers of influence to use their own letterhead (if possible) when sending these appointment-setting letters.

Sample letter that centers of influence can send to their friends and associates — preferably on their own letterhead.

Dear [Name]:

I have been a longtime contributor to The Raskin Museum for several reasons:

✓ Raskin holds an important place in our community's and our state's history.

✓ The Raskin Museum provides cultural opportunities that enhance the quality of life in the surrounding region.

✓ The museum continues to give future generations a greater sense of pride in our region's heritage.

This important community asset would not exist were it not for the generosity of many individuals and businesses. And I know first hand of some of the exciting plans that are in the works for the months and years ahead.

[Name], I would be very grateful if you would allow Mark Heistercamp and me to meet with you briefly sometime during the next couple of weeks to tell you more about the museum and share some of the exciting plans that are in store for the months ahead. I promise we'll take no more than a half hour of your time.

I'll give you a call in a few days to set up a time and day that works best for you.

Thanks in advance, [Name], for your willingness to meet with us.

Yours truly,

Jim Thompson

Teach Volunteers How to Set the Appointment

To help board members and volunteers become effective gift solicitors, begin by sharing techniques for setting appointments with would-be donors. Here's some of what should be reviewed with volunteer solicitors:

1. When setting an appointment by phone, be direct in sharing the reason for the proposed visit.

2. Be prepared to overcome possible objections (see box, right). For instance, if the prospect says now is not a good time, ask if you can call back in a couple of weeks or a month.

3. Be willing to say no to a smaller gift on the phone and set an appointment to discuss a larger gift in person. For example, if someone able to give $100,000 says (on the phone) he is willing to give $5,000, politely say no, point to the campaign's significance and need to discuss that effort face to face.

Overcome Donor Objections

In preparing volunteers to set appointments with would-be donors, share comebacks to help overcome donor objections, including:

- I'm too busy right now.
- The timing isn't good.
- I have outstanding pledges at other charities.
- Let me just make a pledge over the phone.
- Our corporate giving committee handles that.
- I'm really not that close to that organization.
- Send me the literature and I'll think about it.
- Business is slow.

Prepare Board Members, Volunteers for Team Solicitations

Before asking board members or other volunteers to participate in donor solicitation calls, know the roles everyone will play, says Marion Conway, principal, Marion Conway Consulting (Verona, NJ).

"Does the board member/volunteer represent the link to the potential donor as a friend, business associate or alumni of the same college, or does he or she represent an added representative from the organization?" Conway says. "Their role may be different depending on their relationship with the potential donor."

In either case, board members/volunteers should share with the prospect their connection with the organization and passion for its mission, their personal relationship with its work and events, how it benefits their family and the community.

Discussing major goals of the strategic plan and the vision for the organization's future is also valuable and appropriate, Conway says.

Meet in advance of the solicitation call to discuss these roles so there are no surprises at the call, she says. Cover the type of questions they will answer, and which questions you will handle: "For example, if you have developed a list of program options that the donor might support, the board member or volunteer may help figure out which options are most likely to appeal to the donor."

If the board member/volunteer has a personal relationship with the potential donor, it is appropriate for him or her to make the ask, says Conway, because it can be done in an informal and personal way. "If the board member/volunteer does not have a personal relationship with the donor, it is better for you to make the ask. In either case you should know what the specific ask will be."

Source: Marion Conway, Marion Conway Consulting, Verona, NJ. Phone (973) 239-8937. E-mail: mc@marionconwayconsulting.com. Website: marionconwaynonprofitconsultant.blogspot.com

---

Prepare for Team Solicitation

If you're making calls in teams of two or three — one staff person and one or two volunteers — be sure the secondary solicitors are fully prepared.

As helpful as it can be to have a team rather than one person make the call, an unprepared team member can unintentionally dismantle what's been accomplished.

Avoid having a team member who:

- Fails to listen fully to the prospect.
- Has little or no background information about the prospect.
- Has yet to make a generous commitment to your organization.
- Talks too much.
- Lacks understanding about the project you wish to have funded.
- Isn't familiar with key facts or the history of your organization and its work.
- Has little or no previous involvement with your organization.

Train Volunteers To Ask for an Amount

Experienced development professionals know it's best to ask prospects for a specific dollar amount when soliciting a gift. But volunteers often struggle with this. It's out of their comfort zone.

To help reluctant volunteer solicitors ask for a specific gift amount:

- ✓ Tell them to lead by example. Have the volunteer tell the prospect the amount he/she has given or pledged.
- ✓ Suggest that the volunteer share a list of gift opportunities that each have a price tag appropriate for the person being called on to give.
- ✓ Have the volunteer share a list of your gift clubs or ranges so the volunteer can point to the gift club you would like the prospect to consider.

Involving Board Members in Fundraising Process

 How do you retrain existing board members to become more involved in fundraising?

"I have often had to come into an organization and change the rules. Change is threatening and hard, but I like to see an opportunity in every situation. What I have learned over time is that if you introduce change as a mission-driven conversation, it is more likely to be accepted with an open mind, if not embraced.

"If you're going to introduce fundraising as a concept, introduce it with a deep discussion about your mission. Is it possible that as a result of this discussion you might lose some board members? Today, more funders and donors are asking if 100 percent of the board has given, and if they haven't, that will affect your ability to raise gifts."

Source: Jean Block, President, Jean Block Consulting, Inc., Albuquerque, NM. Phone (505) 899-1520. E-mail: jean@jblockinc.com

Teach Board Members to Nurture Relationships

Board members can play a powerful role in making introductions and cultivating relationships on your organization's behalf.

To make them more aware of their potential and assume a more proactive role in making introductions with and cultivating major gift prospects, follow these steps:

1. Regularly share lists of nondonor prospects with board members. Ask them to select names of individuals, businesses and/or foundations they are willing to cultivate in various ways.

2. Share examples of board members or other volunteers who took the time to introduce your charity, particularly those whose introductions eventually resulted in major gifts.

3. Make board members aware that you, or another staff person, are ready and willing to accompany board members on visits to would-be donors.

4. Encourage working in pairs if they find doing so more comfortable or productive.

5. Compliment board members who are performing and producing as expected. Do so in the presence of other board members.

Teach Board Members to Have Fun Soliciting Gifts

Board members will be more eager to assist in soliciting major gifts if they find the experience enjoyable. That's why it makes sense to incorporate fun into your board's solicitation efforts.

The following techniques will help to make board members' asking assignments more pleasant and energizing:

• Invite board members to make calls in teams of two. That makes the task more palatable and strengthens board camaraderie.

• Incorporate some competition among individual board members and board teams (e.g., largest gift solicited, most new pledges during a quarter, most difficult prospect award). Provide regular updates on who's in the lead.

• Make time to celebrate solicitation victories along the way. Recognize individual and team successes.

• Allow time at meetings for board members to share anecdotes of completed calls.

• Mix in thank-you calls with solicitation calls. Thanking donors is rewarding.

• During a training session, conduct a demonstration of the right way and wrong way to solicit a major gift. Have fun with this, incorporating humor into the example of what not to do.

Report Form Helps Solicitors Fulfill Expectations

When enlisting board members and volunteers in gift solicitation, be sure to provide them with an easy-to-understand form they can use to fulfill what's expected of them.

Although you will no doubt send marketing materials, pledge forms and perhaps additional information with them on prospect calls, note that a prospect profile and solicitation report such as the template shown here will provide key information about the prospect and help volunteer solicitors stay on track throughout the solicitation process.

PROSPECT PROFILE AND SOLICITATION REPORT
— FOR INDIVIDUALS —

Lead Solicitor _____
Secondary Solicitors_____
Prospect _____
Home Address_____
City _____ State _____ ZIP _____
Home Phone _____ E-mail _____
Business _____ Title _____
Business Address _____
Business Phone _____ E-mail _____
Spouse _____
Relationship to [Name of Charity] _____

5-YEAR HISTORY OF CONTRIBUTIONS TO [NAME OF CHARITY]

YEAR	AMOUNT	PURPOSE
2007	$5,000	Unrestricted (Annual Fund)
2008	$7,000	Unrestricted (Annual Fund)
2009	$7,000	Unrestricted (Annual Fund)
2010	$7,500	Unrestricted (Annual Fund)

Amount to be Solicited $ _____

SOLICITATION RESULTS
Date of Solicitation _____
☐ **Yes** Amount $ _____ Form of Gift_____
If pledged, over what period of time? _____
Beginning _____ Ending _____
Use of gift _____
☐ **No** Reason:_____
☐ **Decision Pending** Planned Follow-up:_____
Additional Comments Regarding Prospect: _____

Please use back of form to record key discussion points of call. Return to [Name of Organization]

Create a Top-drawer Group of Major Gift Solicitors

It's not necessary that you have a large major gifts committee made up of willing solicitors. It is important, however, that you build a capable and accomplished group of volunteer solicitors.

Take a long-term approach to educating and training those involved with fund development. Meet regularly with them and use varied approaches to train them to be the best solicitors around. Spoon-feed your volunteers using these teaching methods:

1. Take volunteers along on solicitation calls in which you play the key role. Let them see you in action and learn from your style and technique.

2. Invite volunteers to accompany you on thank-you calls and instruct them to take a more active role in the conversation.

3. Conduct mock interviews in the presence of your volunteers. Include a team of two solicitors (one staff and one volunteer) who pretend to introduce themselves to or cultivate or solicit a prospect (also played by a volunteer). Conduct a 10-minute mock interview each time your group meets, involving a different scenario each time.

4. Put out a weekly memo to your volunteer team that educates, offering solicitation tips and techniques — phrases used to overcome objections, phrases used to close gifts, etc.

5. Keep educating your volunteers with useful information about your organization that will equip them to better sell your cause and make them more confident when approaching others — facts such as your organization's annual budget, payroll, available services and programs, greatest accomplishments, greatest challenges and so forth.

6. When you meet as a group, discuss completed calls and strategies for upcoming calls to learn what's working best.

Equip Volunteer Callers With Solicitation Summary Reports

What documentation do you provide volunteers to help them make effective calls on your charity's behalf?

Volunteers and board members can be very instrumental in soliciting gifts of all kinds — annual, major gifts, planned gifts and more. Their effectiveness, however, is a measure of how well-equipped they are before, during and after a call is made.

The solicitation summary report at right serves as a valuable tool for volunteer solicitors. The one-page tool is intended to:

1. Provide a concise summary of the prospect along with his/her recent giving history.
2. Give specific instructions regarding the type of call to be made.
3. Encourage the caller to record when the call was made, what took place and what follow-up steps should occur.

Although volunteers and board members involved in the solicitation process should receive appropriate training prior to making calls, the solicitation summary report becomes an important tool both prior to and following the call. Prospect profile information and instructions are valuable to the volunteer, and comments and follow-up advice are useful to staff and future volunteers involved with a particular call.

The following information is intended to help you better instruct volunteers as to the form's use:

1. **Prospect profile** — basic information intended to help the volunteer understand the individual's relationship with the charity and establish rapport with him/her.
2. **Objective** — provides a clear statement of expectation for the volunteer.
3. **Call outcome** — volunteer summarizes the call: To what degree the stated objective was met, along with any comments that may provide insight into the prospect's decision.
4. **Follow-up** — describes what steps should be carried out (and when) in the future, based on the call's outcome.
5. **Volunteer's signature and date** report is turned into the charity's office.

SOLICITATION SUMMARY REPORT

Prospect Name _____ Title_____

Organization _____

Address _____

Phone (W)_____ (H)_____

Relationship to [Name of Charity] _____
_____

Solicitation Target_____

Recent Giving History _____

Objective of Call_____

Name of Solicitor _____

Date of Call_____ Duration of Call _____

Met with Prospect
❏ Office   ❏ Residence   ❏ Other _____

Summary of Call's Outcome _____
_____
_____

Recommended Follow-up_____
_____
_____

_____   _____
SIGNATURE OF SOLICITOR   DATE

Thank-you Calling Campaign Involves, Inspires and Educates Board Members

Board members at SHALVA (Chicago, IL) — a nonprofit that provides domestic violence counseling services to the Jewish community — regularly call donors to say thanks.

"I think it is impossible to thank donors too much for supporting SHALVA's programs, especially given the current fundraising environment," says Ava Newbart, director of development. "These simple thank-you calls are a great opportunity for SHALVA to personally connect with donors. They are also a way to inspire our board to keep fundraising and promoting SHALVA to our community."

Since SHALVA's office has only four phone lines and a small budget, Newbart asks board members to call donors on their own.

For their first calling campaign, board members called all year-end donors of $50 or more. Newbart e-mailed board members a script, call report form and a list of names with phone numbers. Each board member was asked to make an average of 20 phone calls, for a total of approximately 400 calls.

Newbart followed up with board members via e-mail, encouraging them to make their calls and send her back the forms. "One board member e-mailed me back and asked, 'You want me to call, say thank-you and not ask for anything else? Are you sure?'" she says. "I reassured her, and other board members, that their phone calls would be well received and that they would be happily surprised at donors' responses."

She also reminds board members that with the economy as it is, SHALVA must reach out and personally contact donors; that it's much easier to keep current donors than to find new donors; and that the need for SHALVA's services is on the rise.

For other nonprofits considering starting a simple thank-you campaign, Newbart advises: "Just do it and keep it simple. Being a one-woman shop is challenging. We've talked about making personal thank-you calls for a long time, but there were always competing priorities. Given the climate, our board was open to trying new strategies. Keeping our donors happy is an agency-wide mantra."

Source: Ava Newbart, Director of Development, SHALVA, Chicago, IL.
Phone (773) 583-4673. E-mail: anewbart@shalvaonline.org

Two tools that staff with SHALVA (Chicago, IL) provide to board members to make donor thank-you calls are the call report, below, and informational sheet with sample scripts, at right.

Content not available in this edition

The Conversation:
The intention of your call is ONLY to thank donors for their gifts received.

Sample Opener:
"Hello, Mr./Mrs. X. My name is Jane Brown and I'm a member of the volunteer board of directors of SHALVA. I am calling to thank you for your support of our organization. We received your recent gift and I wanted to let you know, personally, how very much we appreciate it."

At this point, simply pause and wait for a response. Some donors are quite startled and don't know what to say. Usually, they are very appreciative and gracious.

Most calls are very short, simply ending after you express your thanks. Please do NOT make any comment that could be construed as another request, such as "We are grateful for your gift and hope you will continue to support us in the future." This hints of another solicitation, and we want to avoid leaving that impression.

Sample Closer:
You can end the call by simply wishing the donor a pleasant evening.

Sometimes a caller will ask you about how SHALVA is doing or will want some information about our programs and services. If you are comfortable answering their questions, by all means do so. If not, perhaps you could ask if they would like a staff member to contact them separately. If so, please let us know. If a donor expresses an interest in giving more or in volunteering time, you can definitely engage in that discussion. Other organizations' experience with thank-you calls by board members has shown that a small number of donors want to discuss making an additional gift and sometimes it can be significantly higher than the gift they have recently made.

What happens as a result of these calls? Donors who receive a personal call (including those who received messages left on answering machines) will be specially coded by the office, and any additional information gathered during the calls will also be recorded.

The next time these donors are solicited along with other donors who did not receive a call, we will be able to compare their average gift levels, their rate of response, the promptness of response and other information. We can continue to compare these groups for a couple of years, which will allow us to measure long-term loyalty of the two groups. Though we anticipate that donors who receive personal calls are likely to show greater loyalty over time and make increasingly generous gifts, we need reliable information from this test for future planning and forecasting.

How to Harness the Power of Volunteers, Board Members in Fund Development

INVOLVEMENT THROUGH COMMITTEES AND ADVISORY GROUPS

Recognize the many and varied ways of involving volunteers and board members in fund development. Establish a system for tracking volunteer involvement that allows you to evaluate levels of engagement and moves volunteers toward progressively higher levels of involvment, the highest level being that of board member.

Active Committees Give Way To Increased Support

It's a basic fund development premise: Meaningful volunteer involvement results in financial contributions. So, doesn't it make sense that the more you involve volunteers in meaningful ways, the more you will eventually increase both annual and major gifts?

Here's a checklist of some of the types of committees and advisory groups volunteers can join to expand their involvement in fund development:

- ❑ Board Development
- ❑ Major Gifts
- ❑ Planned Gifts
- ❑ Phonathon
- ❑ Auxiliary
- ❑ Public Relations
- ❑ Rating and Screening
- ❑ Grants & Foundations
- ❑ Membership
- ❑ Endowment
- ❑ Memorial/In Tribute Gifts

- ❑ Annual Fund
- ❑ Campaign Steering
- ❑ Planning Task Force
- ❑ Special Events
- ❑ Strategic Planning
- ❑ Nominating
- ❑ Special Gifts
- ❑ Community Campaign
- ❑ Giving Clubs
- ❑ Awards

Spell Out Committee Goals

It's impossible to nurture a can-do committee of volunteers unless they know what's expected of them. Whether you call it a development committee, an annual fund committee or some other name, make expectations clear. To do that:

✓ Share a committee responsibilities description during the recruitment process to avoid any surprises.

✓ Prepare and distribute a yearlong calendar of meeting dates and other crucial events and deadlines.

✓ Instruct your committee chair to make individual assignments to members at each meeting. Include deadlines.

✓ Follow up all meetings with a written memo that confirms individual assignments and deadlines.

✓ Regularly recognize (in the presence of others) those who follow through on assignments in a timely way.

Business Advisory Council Helps Multiply Business Gifts

Why should you take precious time to form a business advisory council? Because council members' willingness to become involved can increase business gift revenue dramatically.

If you're just getting started, begin by reviewing your existing list of business and corporate contributors. If you want to form a group of up to 10 individuals who will meet quarterly, identify 20 prospective members — knowing your request to become involved will be declined by some — and prioritize them according to who you think would make the best council members. Then, develop a written job description for the group and begin setting individual appointments to make your case and share your written expectations.

Here are some duties your business advisory council members can take on once the group is formed:

- Review lists of current donors and agree to make individual thank-you calls.
- Review lists of nondonors and divvy out who calls on whom.
- Provide insight into companies' top management and who calls the shots when it comes to contributions.

- Invite business prospects as guests to some of your charity's functions.
- Coordinate a golf classic aimed at those in the business community.
- Design cultivation strategies for businesses capable of major gift support.
- Host monthly power breakfasts that include a brief program on behalf of your organization.
- Help to identify sponsorship opportunities for your charity's programs and match them with potential sponsors.
- Promote your cause to the public through their own businesses (e.g., notices with bank statements, store front posters, promotions that give a percentage of sales to your charity).

Although the business advisory council may describe a wide variety of possible duties, focus the group on the top two or three tasks that will provide them with a true sense of accomplishment as they complete their first year.

Advisory Boards Welcome Involvement, Lead to Major Gifts

Identify and mine specific ways to connect individuals, businesses and industries to your organization to engage them in your cause.

Purdue University (West Lafayette, IN) hosts 34 industrial advisory boards that share research with corporate partners and build relationships that lead to funding.

Each advisory board is tied to a different field of research, such as food sciences, computer science, engineering education, and computer information and technology, says Betsy Liley, assistant vice president for corporate and foundation relations.

Liley says many of the boards are structured around membership levels, which range from $2,500 to $80,000 per year. Average group size is 15 to 20. These annual gifts help pay for the costs of running each board, including a salary for a paid staff member.

In addition to the annual membership gift, many companies sponsor research projects and fund scholarships for students in fields of interest to their advisory board, Liley says. While individual board structures vary, generally, each board sponsors research as a group, attends two meetings a year and may participate in annual job recruitment fairs.

"If the company's interest is in students and recruiting, they will be interested in supporting scholarships that will get them in front of students," she says. "If their interest is in research, they will want to sponsor research projects that expose them to our experts and allow them direct access to our research."

Advisory board members are at the corporate management level. Specific departments or colleges — many of which already have relationships with those departments or colleges through previous research funding — identify prospective corporate partners or attendance at job recruitment fairs on campus.

"Corporate involvement helps shape our curriculum, keeps us up to date on the skills our students need to have to compete in the job market, and guides our research," says Liley. "Our corporate partners have access to our research and our top students, and get to interact with their peers and partner with them on projects."

Source: Betsy Liley, Assistant Vice President for Corporate & Foundation Relations, Purdue University, West Lafayette, IN. Phone (765) 494-0635. E-mail: bliley@purdue.edu

Industrial advisory boards at Purdue University (West Lafayette, IN) allow the university to share research with corporate partners.

Content not available in this edition

Content not available in this edition

Advisory Council Members Serve as Strong Advocates

Thirty people of various ages, professions and interests come together to serve as advocates for the Sidney Kimmel Comprehensive Cancer Center at Johns Hopkins (Baltimore, MD).

"The mission is for the (advisory council) members to be knowledgeable, informed advocates for the cancer center," Ellen Stifler, director of development, says of the 9-year-old advisory council.

Members of the elite group advocate for the organization. Some refer friends to the cancer center for care. Others share their knowledge of cancer and the center with colleagues and government officials, spearhead fundraising efforts or assist with donor cultivation and gift solicitation.

"There have been times when a particular council member has come with the director or me on a call, and therefore been an advocate for the mission of the cancer center and for the purpose of the ask," Stifler says. "That also lends a real credibility as peer to peer."

While the advisory council benefits the cancer center, Stifler says, membership on the council is mutually rewarding, as it is also a great way to steward current donors.

"It is wonderful stewardship for people who care about the cancer center's mission," Stifler says. "They learn a lot. It is very educational. Additionally, people like to be connected with the leadership of the Kimmel Cancer Center. It brings them into the family."

To create a successful and productive advisory council, remember, "The most important thing is the people you bring in," she says. "Be very careful in selecting the right people. They should be eager for new ideas, have new ideas and respect the director's plans." Additionally, "Be willing to rethink and continually work to improve the council."

Source: Ellen Stifler, Director of Development, Sidney Kimmel Comprehensive Cancer Center at Johns Hopkins, Baltimore, MD. Phone (410) 516-4262. E-mail: stifler@jhu.edu

---

Motivate Advisory Council Members

Ellen Stifler, director of development, Sidney Kimmel Comprehensive Cancer Center (Baltimore, MD), says she considers the cancer center's advisory council to be strong.

However, its members recently encountered a challenge, when its well-respected and well-liked director died of cancer.

"Our challenge has been to keep our council members interested and invigorated," Stifler says. "It was our goal to maintain momentum even when we all missed our former director. We added new members, and we are continually working to reinvigorate and improve the meetings and interactions."

For example, the council, which meets biannually, will now rotate meeting locations, such as meeting in the kitchen of the cancer center's new patient and family pavilion taking a private tour.

Stifler also plans to make meetings more interactive rather than show and tell. She is planning a four-member panel discussion with experts from the cancer center talking on cancer prevention and control, allowing ample time for questions and conversation.

Feed Your Development Committee Fundraising Choices

Some development committees never quite get off of dead center when it comes to raising funds. Others tend to become stagnant because they don't become energized by fundraising options.

To help your development committee create and maintain momentum, keep feeding the members fundraising options when they meet. Here are a few examples you can share with your committee:

✓ Conduct a telesolicitation effort near fiscal year-end directed to those who have yet to fulfill their annual pledges.

✓ Make personal thank-you calls on any local businesses that contributed a minimum gift within the past month or quarter.

✓ Review lists of nondonors to formulate solicitation strategies and decide who would be best to solicit a gift.

✓ Host periodic receptions for prospective contributors.

✓ Help coordinate an estate planning seminar.

✓ Sign a direct mail appeal aimed at a particular group of prospects.

✓ Plan and coordinate a special event — golf classic, silent/live auction(s) or sports banquet designed to raise funds and introduce new people to your organization.

✓ Coordinate and run a mini-campaign to raise gifts for a highly popular funding

Nurture Your Development Committee Chair

Just as it's important that you provide ongoing training for your development committee — whether that's a board committee or a separate group — it's equally important that you make time to train and nurture the person chairing that committee. Here are some ways to do that:

1. Review historical gift data so the chair knows who is giving and at what levels.

2. Share key challenges/opportunities facing your department for the current and upcoming year.

3. Review your most recent year's fundraising strategies (e.g., direct mail, phonathon, face-to-face calls) to help him/her get an understanding of what's being done.

4. Present your top five ideas on ways the development committee can make a meaningful impact in supporting your department's objectives.

After following these steps, allow and invite your chairperson to help shape a plan of action.

Train Chapters to Raise Funds on Your Behalf

The saying goes, "Give a man a fish and you feed him for a day; teach a man to fish and you feed him for a lifetime."

That same principal applies to teaching chapter members to raise funds in their communities on your behalf: If you invest the time to train them, you will have invested in the overall success of the chapter itself, as well as benefits the chapter can bring to your organization.

Helping chapter members raise funds in their own communities on your behalf (rather than you attempting to do so long-distance) just makes sense. They know the territory and, if willing and properly trained, are in a far better position to raise funds than someone not from the area.

To train chapter leaders to raise funds for your organization:

1. Provide templates for direct mail appeals that they can tailor to their particular needs. With templates in hand, they can produce letters, sign them, stuff and mail the appeals.

2. Train one or two people willing to organize a volunteer-driven phonathon. Those chairs can then recruit and train volunteers willing to make phone calls. Provide them with templates of scripts, caller cards, step-by-step procedures and more.

3. Invite chapter leaders to organize special events in their communities. Give them examples of fund raisers from which they can choose.

4. Conduct a training session for each chapter on procedures and techniques for making personal calls on individuals and businesses. Organize teams and include time for practice solicitation. Provide handouts of brochures, pledge forms and such they can take with them.

Give Your Auction Committee Some Direction

Both silent and live auction items can either add excitement (and lots more revenue) to an event or they can contribute to a humdrum experience for your guests.

To be sure your auction committee members are going after donated items that will spark attendees' interest, give these foot soldiers some direction and ideas:

1. **Start early.** Ask committee members to start early in seeking hard-to-get donations (e.g. celebrity made or autographed items, pricey items that may require head office approval).

2. **Go for unique higher-end items.** Don't mimic every other special event's live auction items. Encourage committee members to connect with affluent or influential individuals to come up with items that can't be purchased in a store: tickets to be guests on Oprah, a celebrity hunting excursion, a one-week stay at an oceanfront home.

3. **Create themed packages.** Rather than displaying single items for bidding, group items into themed packages that will add value and fun to the bidding: Baseball Enthusiast's Escapade, Chocolate & Coffee Ecstasy and more.

Start a 'GOG' Club for Most Loyal Givers

You've probably heard how board members should be expected to "give or get" sufficient levels of support to justify their participation on your board. That same concept can work to initiate a club of your most loyal constituents. You could call it the GOG Club (for give or get).

Those persons who join (not limited to board members) would be expected to either contribute at a certain level each year or find other contributors whose gifts will total that amount or more.

Let's say, for example, your GOG Club members are expected to each come up with $2,500 per year. That means they each pony up that amount or they solicit gifts totaling or exceeding $2,500 each year.

To continue to build a club of supporters at that level, ask for members' assistance in coming up with member benefits that will help motivate their participation.

Form a Volunteer-driven Sponsorship Committee

To increase revenue from sponsorships, why not establish a sponsorship committee whose members meet periodically and enlist new sponsors for current and new projects?

Having a sponsorship committee accomplishes several positive goals. For example:

1. It allows you to make more sponsorship contacts than you could ever hope to do on your own.

2. It increases your odds for success since committee members may have greater leverage in securing some sponsorships.

3. The committee can help return current sponsors by having them serve on the committee.

4. It offers another volunteer involvement opportunity in fund development efforts.

Use this sample description as a tool to set up your own sponsorship committee:

SPONSORSHIP COMMITTEE MEMBERSHIP AND RESPONSIBILITIES

The primary purpose of the Sponsorship Committee is to help generate additional revenue for [Name of Organization] through new and renewed sponsorships. The Committee is also charged with evaluating all aspects of the sponsorship program and making recommendations to the Development Office.

Committee Membership

The Sponsorship Committee shall include no less than six individuals, at least three of whom shall represent current or past sponsors. Committee members shall serve a term of at least two years.

Committee Responsibilities

1. Sponsorship Committee members will meet no less than quarterly.

2. Committee members will meet to:

   A. Review existing names of potential sponsors and identify new prospects.
   B. Determine which committee members will contact particular sponsor prospects.
   C. Work with current sponsors to ensure compliance with sponsorship agreements (e.g., sponsor benefits, etc.).
   D. Work with Development Office personnel to identify new sponsorship opportunities at [Name of Organization].
   E. Determine stewardship actions to be taken with current sponsors.
   F. Review procedures and policies related to sponsorships and make recommendations.

Cultivate Neighborhood Ambassadors

If your charity relies on the financial support of community residents, it may be worth your while to develop neighborhood strategies.

Here are some examples from which to develop your own set of actions:

1. Divide your community into neighborhoods and identify where your highest concentrations of donors exist.

2. Develop membership benefits for those willing to invest in your cause. Make it enticing for area residents to want to become associated with your cause.

3. Develop advisory committees made up of existing donors for each neighborhood.

4. Test new methods of raising funds in various locations: a solicitation pass kit in one area, a reception and program in another area, a direct mail appeal signed by neighbors in another location.

5. Use the town meeting concept to seek advice from each neighborhood on ways your organization can be more effective in its delivery of services.

6. Figure out various ways of bringing your services or programs or events to each neighborhood prior to asking for support.

Developing a corps of supporters in each neighborhood will create ongoing good will for your cause.

How to Harness the Power of Volunteers, Board Members in Fund Development

ENGAGING VOLUNTEERS AND BOARD MEMBERS IN ANNUAL GIVING EFFORTS

Volunteers and board members can play a vital role in helping your annual fund efforts by: a) retaining previous years' donors, b) expanding your annual base of support and c) upgrading current donors gifts. They can participate in volunteer-driven campaigns, make calls in your phonathon, sign appeal letters, help identify, rate and screen prospects, plan and host events, make referrals, serve on a committee and more. Any organization that's not involving volunteers and board members in their annual fund efforts is missing a valuable opportunity to increase gift revenue.

An Annual Fund Committee Might Be the Ticket for You

Provided you're willing to give it the attention it deserves, an active annual fund committee or membership committee can make a big difference in expanding your donor base and moving donors to higher levels of giving.

Select willing, enthusiastic volunteers from among existing donors as you recruit committee members. Ask them to serve at least a two-year term so you can stagger those coming on and going off the committee from year to year.

Here are ten examples of what your committee can do to reach new levels of annual giving support:

1. Regularly review a list of nondonors with the purpose of selecting names for face-to-face calls.
2. Conduct a telesolicitation effort in which they recruit additional volunteers to phone prospects over a three- or four-day period.
3. Conduct a thank-a-thon with face-to-face and/or phone calls to donors who gave above a certain level during the previous fiscal year.
4. Host individual receptions in their homes (or elsewhere) to introduce your organization to new prospects.
5. Refer names of and make calls on friends, associates and relatives.
6. Organize a new special event that attracts fresh supporters and provides valuable visibility for your cause.
7. Organize a personalized letter-writing campaign in which volunteers write letters to people they know, inviting them to make a first-time gift.
8. Conduct a fourth-quarter effort to contact persons with unpaid pledges, encouraging them to contribute before year-end.
9. Host a kickoff reception at the beginning of your fiscal year complete with a catchy theme and lots of enthusiasm.
10. Coordinate a year-end celebration that thanks annual fund donors and keeps the annual fund visible in the eyes of donors and the public.

Keep Your Annual Fund Committee's Platter Full

An annual fund committee — made up of board members, volunteers or a combination of both — can make a big difference in your year-end success.

If you have not yet assembled a group to assist in your annual gifts program, you have a tremendous untapped source of gifts waiting to be given. If an annual gifts committee already exists at your charity, work to expand the many ways in which board members and volunteers can assist in your fundraising efforts.

Here are some examples of how board members and volunteers can help:

- Review lists of existing donors to determine individual approaches for increased giving.
- Review lists of nondonors to determine who might solicit whom for a first-time gift.
- Invite committee members to develop a list of friends and colleagues to solicit either face-to-face or through written requests using their personal/business letterhead.
- Direct the group to act as a steering committee for a community-wide, volunteer-driven campaign.
- Instruct the committee to host a yearlong series of monthly breakfasts targeting various groups (e.g., Chamber of Commerce members, civic organizations, women).
- Invite the committee to collectively establish an annual fund challenge gift which matches new and increased gifts.
- Charge this group with responsibility for expanding the number of annual donors at the $1,000-plus level.
- Assign committee members with personally thanking previous year's donors above a certain gift level.

The possibilities for volunteer involvement in an annual gifts program is limitless. The more opportunities for involvement you share, the more you can justify expanding your numbers in this group. The bottom line will be increased support for your institution.

Development Committee Needs Annual Goals, Too

As you prepare your operational plan that spells out fundraising goals for the year, be sure to include quantifiable objectives for your development committee. Equally important, encourage development committee members to help develop those objectives. They'll be more focused on achieving goals if they help establish them.

Here are some examples of quantifiable objectives that development committees might have on their platters:

- To make 50 new calls on prospective $1,000 donors throughout the year.
- To approach up to 10 prospects to establish a $50,000 challenge gift.
- To develop a policy statement for the acceptance of in-kind gifts and present it for board approval.

Ask Board Members to Secure $1,000-plus Donors

To broaden your base of future major donors, turn to your board. Ask each board member to identify, cultivate and solicit three annual gifts of $1,000 or more this fiscal year.

Although you or other staff may need to assist each board member in various ways — identification, strategizing, accompanying them on calls — this expectation gets board members to assume greater ownership in fund development. They will, by their very involvement, be more enthusiastic about wanting to achieve fundraising success, and will likely become more committed donors themselves.

> **Do the Math:** 20 board members each securing three gifts of $1,000 or more throughout your fiscal year would result in 60 new $1,000 contributors. That's 60 new donors capable of one day making a major gift.

Create Some Friendly Competition Among Board Members

Want to get your board more actively involved in fund development? Create a friendly competition to see who can make the most asks or raise the most in gifts.

Try it for a four-month period to test its effectiveness.

Pair up board members so they can make calls together, which is more fun than flying solo. Then divide the pairs into two teams. Give awards to the pair that achieves the best results and an award to the overall winning team as well.

Awards need not be expensive. Think of what would most motivate board members: a dinner prepared by your CEO, a gift certificate to a great restaurant, having one of your programs named in their honor for one year or whatever strikes their fancy.

The ultimate goal is to get your board members more involved with and energized about raising funds.

Energize Annual Giving Efforts by Engaging Younger Donors

Times are tough in annual giving; participation rates are dropping and donors are giving to fewer organizations. Meanwhile, the number of nonprofits continues to grow.

The key to gaining new annual commitments may be found in younger donors, says Brian Kish, assistant vice president for advancement at Salve Regina University (Newport, RI) and an annual giving consultant with Campbell & Company (Chicago, IL). While older donors already have their loyalties in place, he says, most Generation X and Y donors are free to be courted.

He suggests a three-pronged approach to attracting and sustaining younger donors:

1. **Make it fun.** "Younger generations of donors want to put the fun back in fundraising. It is important to cater to that need. Go ahead and send out the mailers, call them during your phonathon, but when it comes time for the fundraiser, get creative: throw a party with drinks and music, have a doggie walkathon or a moustache-growing contest. That's how your organization will stand out from the crowd."

2. **Focus on the social.** Where older generations of donors compartmentalized their work, family and civic duties, he says, younger donors are blending their family needs and social needs with philanthropic needs. "This hasn't been done before," says Kish, "and it means focusing heavily on the social, grassroots aspects of engagement. You want people to be asking one another, 'Are you going to this event? Well then so am I.' This is the most effective way to promote to younger donors."

3. **Early engagement.** The earlier you start engaging potential donors, the better, Kish says. At his institution, most donors making gifts of more than $1,000 have been donating under $1,000 for at least 13 years. Kish says that the likelihood of a donor returning to donate to the same institution increases approximately 20 percent with each year he/she is engaged, so the sooner you start that process, the more support your institution can count on in the long run. At Salve Regina University, fundraisers begin engaging members of the senior class well before graduation. "They may not be able to donate until many years after they've left," Kish says, "but if we engage them while they're still here, when they are able to donate, they will think of us."

Source: Brian Kish, Assistant Vice President for Advancement, Salve Regina University, Newport, RI, and Annual Giving Consultant, Campbell & Company, Chicago, IL. Phone (401) 847-6650. E-mail: annualGiving@campbellcompany.com or brian.kish@salve.edu. Websites: www.campbellcompany.com/people/b_kish.html or www.salve.edu

> ### Cutting Annual Giving Could Undermine Long-term Support
>
> Many organizations are including annual giving programs in budget cuts because, on paper, they earn a lower dollar amount per year, says Brian Kish, assistant vice president for advancement at Salve Regina University (Newport, RI) and an annual giving consultant with Campbell & Company (Chicago, IL). But Kish warns against this strategy, comparing the necessity of annual giving to Research and Development in the corporate setting:
>
> "It may seem like the effort of the R&D team is taking a long time to pay off, but when it does, that payoff is huge."
>
> Kish warns that while cutting an annual giving program might save money over the next few years, doing so disables your pipeline of support for the future.

Establish a Cold Calls Committee

To broaden your base of annual support, establish an ongoing cold calls committee made up of loyal supporters willing to meet on a quarterly basis and accept responsibility for making calls between meetings.

Begin by creating a blueprint for your cold calls committee. Some of the responsibilities this committee might assume include:

- Identifying and researching prospects.
- Coordinating a phonathon effort aimed at nondonors.

- Reviewing lists of non-donors to decide 1) cultivation/ solicitation strategies and 2) who should call on whom.
- Offering input on the content of marketing materials targeted to nondonors.
- Offering input on funding projects and/or wish lists aimed at nondonors.
- Hosting one or more open houses targeting nondonors.
- Coordinating a special event aimed at attracting nondonors.

Thorough Solicitation Script Helps Callers Ask for Gifts

To assist volunteers in soliciting annual gifts from their classmates, the office of alumnae/i relations and office of development at Simmons College (Boston, MA) partnered to create a three-page sample script.

The script can be used by callers seeking pledges throughout the year, says Elizabeth Lawton, assistant director for reunion giving, The Simmons Fund.

Created in 2006, the script, which is a part of a leadership guide created for the volunteers, is distributed during the college's Leadership Weekend in October. This event is for all volunteers who give their time and talent to Simmons as class officers, club and regional volunteers, and board members.

The document begins with a simple Making the Ask statement that emphasizes the student caller's important role of encouraging classmates to make gifts to The Simmons Fund through written and personal appeals.

To make it easy for volunteers to use, the script is broken down into sections that follow the natural flow of an ask:

Introduction; Update Records; Establish Rapport; Transition/ Building the Case; and Confirmation/Closing.

The script includes specifics, such as:

- Having the caller identify him/herself as a fellow member of a specific graduating class, mentioning an upcoming reunion and stating that he/she is a class officer.
- Making the case for support that leads into the ask. "We recommend a specific ask for each classmate based on past giving and/or potential," Lawton says.
- Different scenarios of what could happen on the call (e.g., "Yes, I want to make a gift," "I'll think about it," or "No, I do not want to give to Simmons") are included with tips on how to successfully close a gift.
- Additional tips on how to make fundraising calls and what to expect.

Source: Elizabeth Lawton, Assistant Director for Reunion Giving, The Simmons Fund, Simmons College, Boston, MA.
Phone (617) 521-2334. E-mail: Elizabeth.lawton@simmons.edu

How to Identify, Attract Volunteer Callers

Many people shy away from fund raising, so it's often challenging to recruit willing phonathon volunteers. To recruit able and willing callers:

1. **Narrow your pool of likely candidates.** Look for people who are outgoing and comfortable with other people. Find people who are connected in some way to your organization and are passionate about its cause.

2. **Offer incentives and proper recognition.** Give gift certificates to the volunteers who receive the largest pledges, the most pledges, etc. Provide a free meal. Recognize them on your website or in publications. Have

volunteer hours count toward their school's required community service hours.

3. **Advertise.** Emphasize in meetings, on your website, in newsletters, etc. the need for phonathon volunteers. Use a message like, "Come to meet new people, have fun, eat a delicious meal and raise money for a good cause!"

4. **Eliminate the fear.** Offer training and coaching to help volunteers overcome any calling apprehensions. Provide them with necessary information on the organization and why the funds are being raised, so they feel more comfortable making calls.

Advice on Recruiting Volunteer Callers

Does your phonathon rely on the willingness of volunteers to make calls on your behalf? If so, think about making use of these techniques as ways to recruit more callers:

✓ **Offer donated giveaways** (t-shirts, tickets, discount coupons, etc.) as thank you's for those who put in a minimum amount of calling time.

✓ **Offer flexible scheduling.** Allow callers to choose the day, hours and time period they would be willing to make calls.

✓ **Turn to employees.** Get the OK from your executive director or president to give equivalent work time off for any employee who agrees to help.

✓ **Make calling fun.** Set up teams who compete for donated items based on criteria such as largest pledge received, number of pledges received, first-time gifts, etc.

✓ **Approach area clubs** known to take on service projects as a way to enlist groups of callers.

✓ **Initiate a campaign** to encourage existing volunteers to enlist others.

How to Attract 400-plus Volunteer Callers

Attracting several hundred students to make calls for your annual phonathon seems nearly impossible, right?

Not for officials with Luther College (Decorah, IA), who have had an all-volunteer student caller program for 27 years, and who have recruited an average of 400 callers in each of the last 12 years.

Vicki Donhowe, director of development, current gifts, says 70 teams made up of five to 12 student callers each make calls during the 15-night phonathon.

Donhowe shares some of the creative ideas used to recruit and motivate the student callers:

1. **Develop a phonathon theme.** The most recent phonathon's theme, Call of the Wild, includes fun jungle decor and prizes during the phonathon. Organizers incorporate the theme into various publications and events.

2. **Homecoming visibility.** At halftime of Luther College's homecoming football game, phonathon co-chairs perform a skit to recruit more student callers. Donhowe says they also enter in the homecoming parade a float that features theme-appropriate music and costumes to raise awareness for the phonathon.

3. **Personalized thank-you letters.** Prior to the calling nights, the college's vice president of development sends each volunteer a thank-you letter and token which can be redeemed for a prize on their calling night. Donhowe says this incentive helps get the student callers to attend.

4. **Award prizes throughout the calling nights.** Each night of the phonathon, organizers award prizes, including: Luther College logo items, shirts, pens, staplers, travel mugs, clocks, backpacks and more. At the end of the phonathon, they draw for a grand prize (e.g., gas card, Luther College ring valued at $400, iPod, etc.). Each $100 pledge a caller receives equals an entry in the grand prize drawing.

Source: Vicki Donhowe, Director of Development, Current Gifts, Luther College, Decorah, IA. Phone (563) 387-1514. E-mail: donhowvi@luther.edu

Telesolicitation That Includes Volunteer Callers

■ Recruit 30 percent more volunteers for your phonathon than are needed, anticipating not everyone will show up as expected.

■ Space veteran callers next to rookies to help when and if needed. Close proximity also allows new callers to hear how to make contacts with confidence and ease.

■ Whenever a caller receives a pledge for a minimum amount, say $100 or more, add excitement to the calling by rewarding the caller with an inexpensive prize and having his/her name placed in a drawing for a more significant, but donated prize.

Train Callers to Identify Clues to Giving Ability

Whether you do so during your annual phonathon or a phone survey, train callers to ask questions and identify clues to help classify donors' ability to make significant gifts.

Incorporate research questions into the phone conversation as a way to learn more about your constituency. Information that can help profile an individual's capacity to give may include but not be limited to:

- Occupation
- Title
- Personal interests
- Second residence
- Age
- Business and civic involvement
- Circle of friends, associates
- Number/age of children
- Investments
- Location of residence

Instruct callers to record responses once the call is completed. Then be sure to review and follow up with personal contacts whenever key information is recorded.

How to Harness the Power of Volunteers, Board Members in Fund Development

VOLUNTEER ROLES IN YOUR PLANNED GIVING PROGRAM

When it comes to your planned gifts program, don't limit volunteer involvement to a small handful of individuals who serve on your planned gifts committee. There are many ways to engage volunteers, board members and agents of wealth — attorneys, trust officers, CPAs, insurance agents and others — in building your planned gifts program. Involve volunteers in identifying, researching, cultivating, soliciting and stewarding planned gift donors.

Build an Active, Accomplished Planned Gifts Committee

Many nonprofits take the time to form a planned gifts committee that meets occasionally but accomplishes little. That's a waste of everyone's time.

To build an active planned gifts committee, one whose members are really working to help promote and assist with planned gifts activities:

Make expectations clear. Develop a roles and responsibilities statement that sets forth both group and individual expectations for the members of your committee. Review those responsibilities with committee candidates prior to their appointments.

Assist your committee in setting yearly goals that include

quantifiable objectives (e.g., to individually identify and meet with no less than 10 planned gift prospects throughout the year).

Schedule regular meetings that include individual assignments. In addition to reviewing and approving planned gift policies, ask your chair to assign specific tasks to members (e.g. contacting prospects, calling on attorneys, participating in a planned gift seminar).

Give them the recognition they deserve. Devote a page to this group on your website that includes photos and brief biographies. List their names on planned gift letterhead and in your planned gifts newsletter. Publicly introduce them at estate planning seminars and other related events.

Planned Gift Committees Should Include the Creative

Don't limit your planned gift advisory group to attorneys, trust officers, accountants and insurance representatives. Be sure to include less technical persons who might have more creative marketing ideas to offer — public relations or sales specialists, for example.

The addition of nontechnical individuals will help your group look for new and creative ways to market planned gifts and steward those who have already expressed interest in your programs.

Nurture a League of Planned Gift Ambassadors

Although it requires a significant investment of time, building a volunteer group of planned gift ambassadors can significantly increase your ability to identify, cultivate and secure additional planned gifts for your organization.

Here's a framework for building a corps of planned gift ambassadors:

1. **Develop a three-year plan that outlines goals for your ambassador program.** How many volunteers would you like in place at the end of your first year? What communities or geographic locations would be ideal for the presence of these ambassadors?

2. **Methodically begin to recruit, train and support your ambassadors.** Invite those who have already chosen to make a planned gift to serve as ambassadors. Turn to professionals in particular communities who have an existing connection to your cause.

3. **Provide your new recruits with a position description that shows what is expected of them** — to regularly identify, research, cultivate and assist in the solicitation of planned gift prospects.

4. **Work with and support each ambassador and ambassador group as circumstances dictate.** Take an ambassador on a call. Accompany an ambassador who is willing to introduce you to a new planned gift prospect. Meet with a community's ambassador group (which may amount to two or three individuals) to review activities and strategize.

Even if you only have three ambassador groups with three or four members in each group by the end of year one, you will have launched a volunteer effort that will expand and enhance your efforts to market planned gifts.

Engage Volunteers in Planned Gift Development

Whether your planned gifts program is simple or sophisticated, engaging volunteers makes good sense. Anything others can do will multiply your planned gift efforts and increase the probability of receiving more planned gifts. Plus, the very act of involving those individuals will increase the likelihood that they will consider planned gifts as well.

Here are some examples of how to involve volunteers in your planned gifts effort:

❑ **Assemble a planned gifts advisory committee** to review (or create) your planned gifts policies and oversee your program. Include agents of wealth (attorneys, trust officers, accountants, insurance agents), planned gift donors and prospects.

❑ **Enlist small committees in key communities/regions.** Ask participants to serve as ambassadors on your behalf, identifying and cultivating friendships with prospects.

❑ Enlist professionals and friends of your nonprofit to help **conduct an estate planning seminar.**

❑ Ask existing planned gift donors to **write brief articles or offer testimonials** as to why they made the gift. Use in brochures, planned gifts newsletters and at events.

❑ Ask appropriate volunteers or board members to **sign a letter directed to planned gift prospects.**

❑ **Establish a heritage society** coordinated by volunteers to recognize those individuals who have established planned gifts.

Invite Planned Gift Donors to Make Board Testimonials

You'd think that asking members of nonprofit boards to make planned gifts would be like preaching to the choir. But in reality, many nonprofit boards don't set the example they should be expected to when it comes to making planned gifts. If this is the case in your nonprofit, you may want to invite a willing planned gift donor to attend a regular board meeting to explain what motivated him/her to make a planned gift.

In addition to motivating board members to make planned gifts, the presentation of a planned gift donor before your board is a wonderful way to recognize him/her and to formally say "thank you."

You can be sure that those board members who elect to make a planned gift to your organization will be much more qualified to encourage others to consider establishing planned gifts as well.

Nurture Attorney Ambassadors

Anyone with planned giving experience will tell you that having attorneys batting on behalf of your organization is helpful.

But how do you get attorneys on board? After all, attorneys will generally say that ethics prevent them from encouraging clients to make estate plans for a specific nonprofit. And that's true. However, when clients are the ones bringing up the topic of charitable gifts — seeking their attorney's advice — it's in your nonprofit's interest to have attorneys familiar with your cause and the many ways that you accept gifts.

Building a corps of attorney ambassadors is a long-term investment that requires building respect for both you and the institution you represent. With a system in place, you can set annual objectives that include adding and cultivating a minimum number of these professionals to your centers of influence list.

To build an attorney ambassador corps:

• Meet one on one with attorneys in your area to summarize your planned gift program and leave your business card. Stop by at least once a year to update them on your organization and examples of planned gifts you've received.

• Put those attorneys on your mailing list to receive your newsletter, magazine and planned gifts newsletter.

• Be sure your planned gifts advisory committee — and, if possible, board of trustees — include attorneys.

• Cultivate attorney relationships by including them in estate planning workshops for your constituency. If you coordinate workshops in other communities, recruit attorneys from those locations to assist with your effort.

• When you come across a charitable gift article that would interest your attorney ambassadors, send them a copy of it along with a personal note.

• Host a reception or luncheon for your agents of wealth. Have your CEO and other board members on hand to thank them for their interest in your cause. Cite examples of how planned gifts benefit those you serve.

• When your agency realizes planned gifts, don't overlook the attorneys involved in the distribution of assets. They will be much more amiable when future opportunities present themselves if they have had a previously pleasant relationship.

Relationship With Professional Advisors Important

As a planned giving officer, you undoubtedly spend a lot of time with potential donors, as you should. But don't forget the importance of building a solid relationship with professional advisors as well. These agents of wealth may include attorneys, trust officers, financial planners, certified public accounts and even donors' children.

Gary Hargroves, retired director of planned giving, University of Minnesota Medical Foundation (Minneapolis, MN) and now a development consultant, says it's important to develop a strong relationship with this population for three main reasons.

1. **To ensure the gifting process goes smoothly.** Once you have established a relationship with a donor, Hargroves recommends meeting with his or her advisors early on to eliminate the chance of last-minute surprises and questions. "If you get to the advisors early on, you are all playing on the same team," Hargroves says. "Everybody is on the same page when the donor is ready to gift."

2. **To educate.** Hargroves says it's important for professional advisors to have some knowledge of your organization and its credibility. He says they should know that your organization is reputable, treats people right and uses financial gifts responsibly.

3. **To encourage referrals.** Some donors know they want to give to a particular cause, but they are unsure of what organization to give to. Hargroves says that when you have a well-groomed relationship with professional advisors, they are more likely to refer people to your organization. In fact, Hargroves says the Minnesota Medical Foundation typically received at least $1 million from referrals each year.

Source: Gary Hargroves, Development Consultant, Fridley, MN. Phone (763) 242-2228. E-mail: ggh02@comcast.net

Tips to Build a Strong Relationship With Professional Advisors

There are a number of ways to build relationships with professional advisors.

Gary Hargroves, retired director of planned giving, University of Minnesota Medical Foundation (Minneapolis, MN) and now a development consultant, offers these suggestions:

1. **Meet and develop a relationship through your donor.** Request a meeting with your donor and his or her advisors early on.

2. **Send mailings.** An easy way to do this is to utilize the services of companies like R&R Newkirk (Willow Springs, IL). R&R offers customized newsletter mailings. It's a perfect way to keep in touch with professional advisors.

3. **Provide useful information specific to professional advisors on your organization's website.** An example is the resources available on Abbott Northwestern Hospital Foundation's (Minneapolis, MN) site (www.plan.gs/Category.do?orgId=713&contentGroupID=372). This website provides links to several articles and even offers sample bequest language.

4. **Call on professional advisors.** Encourage members of your development team to get to know these agents of wealth. Take them to lunch or buy them a cup of coffee.

5. **Offer teleconferences.** Hargroves says when he worked at the Minnesota Medical Foundation they utilized the services of Crescendo Interactive (Camarillo, CA) and invited professional advisors to quarterly teleconferences with speakers of interest. Typically, 125 attended.

6. **Host a banquet to recognize outstanding professional advisors who made referrals.** Such an event is also the perfect setting to talk about your organization and its mission.

How to Harness the Power of Volunteers, Board Members in Fund Development

ENGAGING FELLOW EMPLOYEES IN FUND DEVELOPMENT

It's easy to overlook fellow employees as volunteers who can become involved in fund development. With a little educating and nurturing on your part, employees outside of the advancement office can become some of your most accomplished ambassadors. Regularly work to make fellow employees more aware of what your department does. Extend an invitation for them to become involved to the extent they are willing. Help them to understand the impact of gifts on your organization and those you serve.

Give Fellow Employees Easy Access to Fund Development

How actively do you invite and encourage fellow employees to assist in your fund development efforts? Do you simply assume they know they are welcome to assist? Or do you have a procedure in place to promote their involvement as centers of influence?

Your colleagues may not realize there are many ways to help beyond soliciting gifts. Also, they need to be made aware of the fact that whatever amount of time they have to give will be welcomed and of value to your organization's cause.

Make use of an involvement form such as the one illustrated here as a way to formalize involvement procedures for employees of your organization.

GLENVIEW SCHOOL
EMPLOYEE AMBASSADOR'S PROGRAM

As an employee of Glenview School, you possess more potential than you may realize when it comes to resources that can enhance our facilities, programs and personnel. The initiative you take to assist our fund development efforts, at whatever level, will assist us in raising additional funds for the school.

Please accept this as your invitation to become involved as a Glenview Ambassador by reviewing these involvement opportunities, indicating your participation interests and returning it to the Development Office at your convenience. Once we hear from you, we will be pleased to visit more about particular involvement opportunities.

Name _____ Date _____

❑ Yes, I want to help. Let's get together and talk specifics.
❑ I might help, but I want to know more first.

Please check your interests here:

_____ Referring names of potential prospects.
_____ Calling on donors to thank them for their support.
_____ Making phonathon calls.
_____ Helping with the annual employee campaign.
_____ Assisting with behind the scenes work (filing, researching, stuffing envelopes, etc.)
_____ Signing appeal letters.
_____ Accompanying development staff on calls.

_____ Hosting a get-together at my home.
_____ Meeting with prospects to tell them more about our programs.
_____ Helping with foundation proposals.
_____ Making a personal gift.
_____ Making a planned gift.
_____ Providing facility tours to prospective donors.
_____ Cultivating relationships with area businesses.
_____ Researching funding opportunities.

Amount of time I am willing to give: _____ Per week _____ Per month

Names of those who might make good prospects for contributions:

Name _____ Address _____
Name _____ Address _____
Name _____ Address _____

I would be willing to:

_____ Tell you more about what I know regarding these referrals.
_____ Help in making an introduction.
_____ Assist in cultivating their interest in Glenview School.
_____ Assist in soliciting them for support.

Five Ways Employees Can Help With Fund Development

Are you doing everything possible to educate your organization's employees about ways they can assist in fund development? After all, they should be more familiar with and more committed to your organization than almost anyone.

Additionally, the more involved nondevelopment employees become in fund development, the more they will come to appreciate the important role your department plays in providing resources for needed programs.

Here are five ways that your colleagues can become more actively involved in fund development:

1. **Setting an example as a regular contributor.** Employees will become more committed to fund development and better at selling your cause if they support the organization personally.

2. **Referring names of potential donors.** There may be prospects who would be prime candidates for major gifts or planned gifts, but until you are made aware of those folks, you can't begin to cultivate them.

3. **Assisting in the cultivation, solicitation and/or stewardship of prospects and donors.** Minimally, employees can make a point to thank current donors for their gifts; this is a good way to ease someone into the fundraising process.

4. **Assume leadership roles in your annual employee campaign.** Peer-to-peer solicitation is much more effective than having development staff approach employees or sending a letter from the president or executive director.

5. **Share achievements with the development staff.** A development officer's ability to excite others about the work of an organization is linked to his/her firsthand knowledge of achievements being made. Other frontline employees should share news of accomplishments with the development office in a timely manner.

With a little encouragement on your part, you may be surprised how other employees begin to work on your behalf and help as centers of influence.

Help Fellow Employees Cultivate Prospect Relationships

To broaden and deepen the level of prospect cultivation at your organization, educate your fellow employees on how they can make introductions and cultivate relationships with would-be donors through their work.

As an example, develop template letters employees can use to write to persons they know and interest them in some aspect of your organization's work. Make it easy for employees to show how they can help by simply corresponding with prospects. When an employee sends a letter of this type, ask that he/she share a copy with your office.

To the right is a sample letter that illustrates how employees can use correspondence as a cultivation tool.

Dear Allison:

Our mass communications department received a grant this past year that has allowed us to expand our writing lab in a number of ways, giving our mass comm students even more opportunities to develop their writing skills. As a graduate of our college who majored in mass communications, I know you would be thrilled to see what this lab is allowing us to do.

I want to invite you to stop by for a visit whenever you get the opportunity to visit our campus again for a personal tour of our lab. I know you will be impressed.

As you might guess, the realization of this lab has set the stage for our next level of expansion, which will do even more to assist today's mass comm students. I can go over these next steps whenever it works for you to pay us a visit.

I hope you'll make a point to visit us whenever you get back to [name of community]. I would love to hear what you've been up to and learn more about your career.

Sincerely,

Margaret Ashbaugh
Dean, School of Communications

Expand Your Donor Base

■ To get more people making annual contributions, ask willing employees to submit names and addresses of family and friends. Then develop a direct mail appeal that invites in tribute gifts honoring any employee's tenure with your nonprofit. This concept can also be retooled to solicit gifts from friends of your volunteers.

Energize Fellow Employees

Want to get nondevelopment employees involved with and energized by fundraising efforts? Meet with each department and discuss their wants and needs for possible inclusion on a rotating wish list that can be shared with those on your mailing list.

Help Employees Cultivate Donors, Would-be Donors

Your organization's employees can become great allies in cultivating prospects and stewarding existing donors. That's why it's important to develop a procedure that fosters employees' involvement in fund development.

To do that:

1. Produce an instructive document you can share with employees on how they can identify, cultivate, solicit and/or steward donors and probable donors.

2. Whenever you have a model employee who has assisted in cultivating or soliciting a major gift, use that example when meeting with other employees. Ask the model employee to share how the experience made a positive difference and to help alleviate other employees' reluctance to become involved.

Many times the synergistic relationship formed by an employee and a donor will bring about a major gift investment that helps that employee's work or department in significant ways.

Produce an instructive document (such as the generic example shown at right) you can share with employees on steps they can take to help with major gift efforts.

How You Can Help With Major Gift Efforts
Prepared for employees of XYZ Nonprofit

Contact any member of the Advancement Department to discuss any of the following ways you can help generate major gifts that will benefit our nonprofit, your departments and those we serve.

Identify major gifts prospects — You may know of individuals, businesses or foundations capable of making major gifts to our agency. Please share their names.

Make introductions and cultivate relationships — If you know or have a relationship with a financially capable individual, business or foundation, your willingness to introduce us or help us build a relationship may serve as the catalyst that results in a major gift.

Assist with solicitation — You don't have to be involved in asking someone for a major gift to become involved with fund development. Just sharing names and/or helping build relationships is enough. However, your willingness to assist in soliciting gifts can be of tremendous help if you choose to do so.

Steward existing contributors — You have no idea how much it helps when an employee thanks a donor for what he/she has done or is doing through their generosity. Helping us share the impact of gifts gives donors the recognition they deserve and also encourages future investments in our agency.

There are so many ways to help us with major gift efforts. Your level of involvement is entirely up to you. Please call or e-mail a member of the Advancement Department to explore how you might help. Thanks for your consideration!

Educate and Train Fellow Employees

Time and effort invested in educating employees outside your development office about major gifts can pay off big through their willingness to identify, cultivate, steward and even help solicit major gifts.

Here are ideas to get your fellow employees more involved in major gifts efforts:

✓ Distribute a twice-monthly e-newsletter or memo to employees sharing what is happening in your office with regard to major gifts: details of funding opportunities, summaries of recent gifts, mention of events they can attend and more.

✓ Ask them to accompany you on calls. There's no better teacher than experience. Their participation will only serve to energize them.

✓ Spoon-feed tasks with which they can help: sharing names, rating and screening prospects, identifying potential funding opportunities and more.

✓ Celebrate and recognize all levels of participation. Keep employees updated on any progress on prospects with whom they have had any level of involvement; make other employees aware of their involvement.

Recognize that nurturing employees takes time, just as it does with board members and other volunteers, but know also that your investment of time will pay off.

Identify and Involve Employees About to Retire

How closely do you monitor the list of retirees from your charity? Those who are retiring may prove to be ideal volunteers for your development shop. Have a procedure in place for identifying and following up with your employees who are about to retire:

1. Meet one-on-one to explore the many ways they could become involved in fund development — prospect cultivation, making calls, prospect research, etc.

2. Suggest a probationary or test period of involvement with an agreed-upon number of hours per week or month so the retiree doesn't become too overwhelmed.

3. If the retiree agrees to give it a go, assign a development staff person to assist, train and fully support the volunteer.

How to Harness the Power of Volunteers, Board Members in Fund Development

TURN TO RETIRED EMPLOYEES, FORMER BOARD MEMBERS FOR HELP

Out of sight, out of mind. Only if you allow that to happen. Retired employees and former board members sometimes turn out to be among the most accomplished volunteers. Because they are recognized and respected by many of your constituents, these individuals can often open doors that others cannot. There knowledge of your organization and people connected with it is also a valuable asset. Look for ways to re-engage these special people in the life of your organization.

Involve Those From Your Past

Are there people from your organization's past — board members, former employees, former clients or members — who are no longer in touch with your organization and its work?

Help bring these potential contributors back by asking for their help. Put a call out for artifacts from your organization's past: old photos, newspaper articles, personal stories, memorabilia and more. Explain that you plan to use the items for an historical display of your organization. Then continue to involve everyone who responds to your request.

Stay Connected With Former Board Members

Developing strong relationships with current board members is key to staying connected with them — and keeping them engaged with and supporting your organization — after they retire.

"There is a greater chance of keeping former board members engaged if they were developed and cultivated during their tenure on the board," says Diane Dean, principal, The Dean Consulting Group (Rutherford, NJ). "There is a unique advantage to having informed insight regarding board members' interests, talents, skills and reasons for committing to the organization on a volunteer leadership level."

Tools to develop and sustain relationships include personal questionnaires, self-assessments and committee evaluations, plus activities at orientations and board retreats.

Forming a board development committee to recruit, engage and develop board members is another useful strategy.

"The best board strategies, the ones that get results that can be tracked to prove success, are those that are incorporated as programs with written procedures and a clear goal of what success looks like," says Paul Nazareth, manager of planned and personal giving, Catholic Archdiocese of Toronto (Toronto, Ontario, Canada).

A well-crafted communications plan should include a formal recognition process for people coming on and off the board.

"One innovative idea I've seen is an organization that will add a recommendation to a board member's LinkedIn profile if he or she fulfills the top five criteria of an excellent board (make a commitment to the board, volunteer in programs, advocate in the community, network for the organization, make a leadership or planned gift)," Nazareth says.

One way to engage retiring board members that is often overlooked is simply to ask them what level of involvement they would like and whether that involvement would occur immediately after the end of their board service or in a few years.

Sources: Diane D. Dean, Principal, The Dean Consulting Group, Rutherford, NJ. Phone (800) 686-1975.
E-mail: ddean@thedeanconsultinggroup.com.
Website: www.thedeanconsultinggroup.com
Paul Nazareth, Manager, Planned and Personal Giving at Catholic Archdiocese of Toronto, Toronto, Ontario, Canada.
Phone (416) 934-3411. E-mail: pnazareth@archtoronto.org.
Website: www.archtoronto.org

Involve Former Chairpersons in Ongoing Idea Sessions

Do you have an annual gift campaign that's volunteer-driven and includes a new chairperson each year?

Rather than retiring those chairs, why not create an exclusive club that includes all former chairpersons?

These people have a wealth of experience and knowledge to offer your organization on an ongoing basis.

Tap this valuable resource. At least once a year, or perhaps quarterly, invite these persons to your organization for a get-together and put them in charge of some ongoing responsibility or brainstorming session that keeps them involved with your fund development activities.

Identify Retirees Who Will Lend Time, Expertise

To expand your major gifts effort, look to retirees who are already committed and contributing to your cause.

Identify, enlist and nurture a small group of individuals who have the background to help advance your work. These volunteers might include:

✓ Former sales executives who know how to sell and aren't reluctant to make the close.

✓ Retired individuals who established large circles of friends and associates: clergy, corporate managers, educators, realtors and more.

✓ Agents of wealth: those whose positions centered around finance — accountants, attorneys, insurance agents and trust officers.

Outline a plan with each volunteer to commit so many hours of development time each week. Provide your volunteers with office space, business cards and other tools that will motivate them and help them achieve success.

Connect With Your Nonprofit's Old Timers

You can learn a lot by meeting with and getting to know your organization's old timers — longtime employees who work for you or may have retired, persons having served on your board years ago, even former donors and volunteers who have faded from active involvement.

By identifying and getting to know them you can:

1. Learn more about your organization's history: its programs and services, accomplishments and more — facts that may uncover information useful to your fundraising efforts.

2. Uncover individual's names who had ties to your organization then but not now.

3. Begin to reconnect and involve these old timers as volunteers and probable donors.

How to Harness the Power of Volunteers, Board Members in Fund Development

ENGAGING VOLUNTEERS AND BOARD MEMBERS IN MAJOR GIFTS EFFORTS

A small handful of connected volunteers and board members can work wonders in realizing major gifts. Those most capable of helping in this area are those who: a) have already stepped up to the plate with significant investments and b) are respected and connected with persons of means. Sometimes they're movers and shakers. Sometimes they're community leaders. And sometimes their positions allow them to regularly rub shoulders with those capable of making significant gifts.

Help Major Gifts Committee Establish a Routine

Chances are you have a major gifts committee that meets from time to time. After all, you need not be in the midst of a capital campaign to justify the ongoing value of such a committee.

To help committee members accomplish as much as possible throughout the year, establish a focused routine of meeting with the committee monthly or quarterly.

Work from a planned agenda that regularly addresses the following topics:

✓ Major gifts realized since the last meeting.

✓ Key prospect names to review and determine next steps.

✓ Discussing completed calls (cultivation, solicitation, stewardship) since last meeting.

✓ Assigning calls to be completed prior to the next meeting.

✓ Additional issues that committee members should be aware of (e.g., strategic planning, new funding opportunities).

Help Your Major Gifts Chair Know What's Expected

While major capital campaigns make a big splash, the pursuit of major gifts must be an ongoing effort, not just something that occurs in a high-profile fundraising effort.

An ongoing major gifts committee will help to ensure that gift getting is a continual process and helps to focus the work of those involved.

Equally important to your success is the selection of your major gifts committee chair. The chairperson's leadership will set the tone and agenda for others' level of commitment to this ongoing process. That's why it's important to develop a job description for this position that can be used in recruiting the right leader and helping him/her to stay on track once he/she has accepted the job.

Develop a job description using this example as a guide:

Role and Responsibilities — Chairperson — Major Gifts Committee

In cooperation with the Office of Institutional Advancement, the chairperson's primary responsibilities include:

1. To first set an example of personal giving for others to follow.

2. To recruit and retain a group of committed volunteers to identify, research, cultivate, solicit and steward major gift prospects and donors.

3. To review policies related to major gifts and regularly provide to the board of trustees reports of major gift progress and offer policy recommendations.

4. To understand, offer input and support the development of the advancement department's yearly operational plan and accompanying master calendar, particularly as it relates to major gifts.

5. To participate in the establishment of forecasts and evaluations of fundraising potential by identifying and rating prospects.

6. To monitor ongoing gift reports and determine future courses of action — in conjunction with advancement staff — based on their results.

7. To provide leadership and assistance to the steering committee and advancement staff during periods of capital campaigns.

8. To work to ensure proper donor and volunteer recognition by thanking and stewarding major gift donors and regularly recognizing those volunteers who assist in the identification, cultivation, solicitation and stewarding of donors.

Get Board Members Involved in Raising Major Gifts

Plot ways to engage key players in your major fundraising efforts to maximize success.

As a way to get board members involved in its campaign, for example, staff with The Clinic (Phoenixville, PA), a medical center for the uninsured, ask board members to handwrite short notes to donors they know.

The notes, written on 2-by-4-inch notepads printed with The Clinic's logo, are included in direct-mail solicitation letters sent to major donors. All board members participate, each writing about a dozen notes.

"Board members may write something positive like, 'We hope you can help us out,' or 'I look forward to seeing you at the next event,'" says Debbie Shupp, development director. "These notes add a personal touch to our mailings."

Board members also write notes to include in event invitations for the major donors they know, says Shupp, who notes: "For our last golf outing, we probably wouldn't have had 80 percent of our sponsors if we did not have board involvement in inviting the sponsors."

Source: Debbie Shupp, Development Director, The Clinic, Phoenixville, PA. Phone (610) 935-1134 ext. 24. E-mail: dshupp@theclinicpa.org

Endowment Committee Brings Focus

Whether you are about to establish an endowment committee of existing donors, board members and/or others, or are looking to fine-tune responsibilities of an existing group, know that an active endowment committee can significantly help raise endowment gifts.

Challenge your endowment committee or endowment advisory group to:

- Develop an endowment acceptance policy.
- Identify endowment gift opportunities.
- Offer formal input regarding the creation of endowment marketing materials.
- Establish named endowment funds of their own.
- Review and contribute to a quarterly newsletter that addresses endowment topics.
- Make cultivation and solicitation calls on prospects.
- Establish stewardship strategies to recognize those who give endowment gifts.
- Establish or provide input for an endowment investment policy.
- Identify strategies promoting endowment among agents of wealth: attorneys, trust officers, CPAs and others.
- Act as a steering committee for an endowment-only campaign.

Focus Centers of Influence On Million-dollar Prospects

With as few as three centers of influence, you can make tremendous headway in identifying and cultivating new million-dollar prospects.

Don't think you have to enlist the help of 20 or 30 centers of influence to make a noticeable difference in discovering and nurturing million-dollar prospects. All it takes is one or two or three committed ambassadors to help your efforts. Time spent educating and supporting a small number of committed volunteers will be far more productive than giving lip service to a larger group who may be far less dedicated.

Train two or three individuals to help you in the following ways:

1. Share methods for identifying individuals with the capacity to make million-dollar gifts.

2. When they do identify prospects, strategize the steps required to make introductions and align your organization with these would-be donors.

3. Keep your centers of influence fully apprised of all plans and actions, just as you would with a fellow development officer.

4. Be prepared to accompany centers of influence on calls or provide them with any additional support that may be of value.

Create a Traveling Ambassador Corps to Assist in Cultivation

Do you have a board member making a business trip to the East or West Coast? What about that retired board member who vacations in Florida each winter?

Turn these and other close friends of your organization into traveling ambassadors by involving them in cultivating major gift prospects who live at or near their travel destinations.

These traveling ambassadors can help do their part to enhance the image and work of your organization throughout the nation.

Use an anticipated trips form such as the one at right to pinpoint opportunities to involve persons in identifying, cultivating, researching and even soliciting gifts on your behalf.

In their travels, these persons could assist you by:

- Hosting a reception.
- Conducting prospect research on individuals, businesses or foundations in that region.
- Making introductory calls.
- Delivering a message of thanks for past support.
- Hand-delivering a proposal.
- Seeking donated items for events.

Rather than sending or e-mailing forms, distribute them at board meetings to explain how helpful involvement can be with these out-of-town prospects. Share the forms selectively on a one-to-one basis with others who travel in affluent circles.

When you receive a completed form, identify appropriate fund development activities and discuss them with the person submitting the form before departure.

Sharing this form will have multiple benefits:

- Completed forms help keep your office posted on the schedules of board members and others.
- By involving these persons in the fund development process, you are also engaging them — helping them more fully own the role of major gifts at your institution.
- Their involvement will help realize cultivation, research and solicitation that otherwise might not have been accomplished.

RANDOM UNIVERSITY
Anticipated Trips Form

This form is for board members and other Random University insiders who wish to serve as ambassadors during their business and leisure travels.

When a trip is planned, simply complete this form and turn in to the Institutional Advancement Office. A development officer will contact you to go over possible ways in which you could assist in making contacts with individuals. Thank you!

Name _____

Trip Destination_____
❑ Business   ❑ Pleasure

Trip Arrival Date_____   Departure Date_____

Where You Can Be Reached During Trip:
Address_____   E-mail _____
Phone (_____)_____   Fax_____

Examples of Ambassador activities with which you might assist:

❑ Introductory visits:
    ❑ With individuals
    ❑ With business representatives
    ❑ With foundations

❑ Friendship-building activities
❑ Distributing literature about Random University
❑ Hosting a reception
❑ Identifying potential contributors
❑ Telephoning friends/donors of the university
❑ Soliciting a gift
❑ Delivering a proposal
❑ Securing donated items for our annual gala
❑ Other (Please describe)_____
_____
_____
_____
_____
_____
_____

Volunteer Recruitment Idea

When enlisting volunteers to assist with major gift solicitation, recruit those who have already made sacrificial stretch gifts. Those who give to their fullest capacity, regardless of amount, will be better at promoting your cause than those who do anything less.

Link Traveling Ambassadors With Faraway Prospects

Take a look at your donor list. Which persons on the list travel for business or personal pleasure on a regular basis?

Why not develop a plan to involve these traveling friends as ambassadors for your organization? Invite them to link up with both prospects and donors who live far from your institution. Properly trained, these traveling ambassadors can assist with identifying, researching, cultivating, soliciting and stewarding faraway constituents.

Follow this step-by-step process to secure and train traveling ambassadors:

1. Enlist two or three existing donors who travel regularly and would be willing to serve as ambassadors on behalf of your organization.

2. With this core committee, review a list of other donors who travel and devise a plan to approach them to determine if any would be willing to join your committee of traveling ambassadors.

3. As your committee grows, meet monthly or quarterly to review names of faraway prospects and donors based on geographic regions. As individual committee members indicate their intent to visit particular cities or regions, invite them to phone or visit face-to-face with persons from those areas. As committee members agree to make calls, outline specific objectives for each person with whom they plan to meet (e.g., thanks for a previous gift, update on happenings at your charity, etc.).

4. Following each meeting, send individual memos to each committee member who reconfirms who he/she is to call on, when, and the objective of the call. You can provide additional background information on those to be seen with this memo. Also include trip report forms (and any additional materials for the ambassador to distribute to prospects/donors).

5. Instruct ambassadors that their completed trip reports include any follow-up to be conducted by your office. You may discover as a result of the visit, for instance, that the timing would be appropriate for solicitation, or a family member's death requires a gesture of sympathy from your nonprofit. The completed trip report will point out what needs to happen next.

6. Finally, as your committee continues to meet, keep members informed on the status of those with whom each has visited. Doing so will help to keep them motivated as owners of the solicitation process.

Develop a form such as this to review names of prospects/donors and determine who will call on whom during the next three-month period.

COMMITTEE OF TRAVELING AMBASSADORS

Long-distance Donors/Prospects To Be Seen

Name	City/State	Relationship	Proposed Objective	Caller	Target Date
M/M Mark Andrews	Cleveland/OH	Prospect/'55 Alum	Rate/screen for major gift	Wilson	02/10
Sarah Gailey	Cleveland/OH	Son attended Postum/Donor	Thank for past support	Wilson	02/10
GoMark Inc./Sands	San Diego/CA	'62 Alum/Donor	Update on scholarship	Hadley	03/10
Bremer Foundation	San Diego/CA	Prospect	Intro/secure guidelines	——	
Allison/Mike Gentry	San Diego/CA	'71/'71 Alums/Donors	Thanks for recent gift	Hadley	03/10
Dr. Claude Everist	San Diego/CA	Emeritus Board Member	Update on strategic plan	Hadley	03/10
Ian Smith	Los Angeles/CA	Former Student/Prospect	Research	——	
Mattie Christensen	Riverside/CA	'43 Alum/Planned Gift	Thank and update	Nelson	02/10
Tom Eisenburg	Los Angeles/CA	'49 Alum/Donor	Solicit for Annual Fund	Nelson	02/10
Melony/Tim Winchell	Kansas City/MO	'72/'74 Alums/Prospects	Share wish list	Hinton	01/10
Hallmark Foundation	Kansas City/MO	Prospect	Intro/secure guidelines	Hinton	01/10
Tina Marie Noonan	Liberty/MO	Former Student/Prospect	Intro/research	Hinton	01/10

How to Harness the Power of Volunteers, Board Members in Fund Development

INVOLVING VOLUNTEERS AND BOARD MEMBERS IN YOUR CAPITAL CAMPAIGN

The most successful capital campaigns engage volunteers and board members in very focused ways over a specified period of time. This more intense, highly structured fundraising effort includes clearly-defined roles and responsibilities for everyone involved. Proper training is essential for those involved in soliciting gifts.

Unlock Your Board's Campaign Potential

Knowing board gifts can account for a third or more of a capital campaign goal, and recognizing that board support establishes the precedent for gifts to follow, what steps can and should you take to prepare board members for unprecedented campaign gifts?

Assuming you already have a board in place that includes financially capable trustees, here are some top recommendations from The Major Gifts Report's panel of experts for encouraging those board members to give at their full potential:

1. **Be sure board members are part of ongoing strategic planning process.** If they are to commit to an ambitious and successful campaign, they need to own the entire process that leads up it. Include them — collectively and individually — in designing a long-term plan for your organization. Help them understand the need for additional resources and what the realization of those resources can accomplish.

2. **Make board members aware of what other successful nonprofits have achieved.** To help raise the sights of your board, share examples of what other charities have accomplished with campaigns. The more examples they see, the more they will understand that they, too, can do the same.

3. **Include lofty goals in your pre-campaign vision.** If you think small, your board will do the same. Instead, everyone needs to reach for goals that will stretch them beyond what they believed capable of themselves. Board members need to believe that the identified goals are critical and must be

achieved to adequately fulfill the organization's mission. You can always pare back goals if necessary, but it's nearly impossible to expand them once a strategic plan has been established.

4. **Cultivate key board members' attention prior to feasibility study.** A feasibility study's results — based on individual and group interviews that include board members — determine the final campaign goal. So it's important before your feasibility study to cultivate individual interest in the campaign with board members whose financial ability can set a precedent. Meet one-on-one to measure both interest in the campaign and in specific giving opportunities. Develop a sense of those persons' potential interests before the feasibility study. Convince them that the magnitude of an eventual campaign will be determined, in part, by the example they set.

5. **Approach board members sequentially based on both gift capability and inclination to give.** Once the feasibility study has been completed and a goal recommended to the full board, approach first those few board members whose sacrificial pledges will send a clear signal to others that this campaign is more significant than any previous effort in the organization's history.

Many facets of the pre-campaign phase are important, but if your board members cannot become passionate about the effort and their individual responsibilities in making it a success, it might be best to rethink your plans.

Focus Groups Prove to be Valuable Pre-campaign Tool

Supporters of the Staunton Performing Arts Center (SPAC) of Staunton, VA, are looking to renovate and restore its Dixie Theatre. To create community awareness and buy-in prior to launching the $9.8 million campaign, they first conducted a series of focus groups in the small community.

Judy Mosedale, executive director, says the focus groups provided insight into the public's knowledge and understanding of the project and helped inform the public that their input into the proposed restoration was welcome — which helped to create buy-in that will hopefully lead to contributions.

This basic information regarding Staunton's focus groups can serve as a reference when planning your organization's focus groups:

- **What:** Four focus groups held at local library. Dates and times varied to accommodate as many people as possible. Each focus group lasted 90 minutes.

- **Attendees:** Twenty-seven people participated. "We made a pubic appeal, and the participants self-selected," Mosedale says. SPAC sent e-mails to those on its e-mail list,

submitted press releases to the media and hung posters in the community.

- **Facilitator/Recorder:** A professional facilitator asked eight main questions. (In this case, the facilitator happened to be a board member.) Additional probing questions were asked to spark conversation and clarify responses. Mosedale served as the recorder.

- **Planning:** Mosedale and members of the board of directors' strategic planning committee were responsible for planning the focus groups. Mosedale and the facilitator developed the questions.

- **Results:** The facilitator presented a written report to the board of directors. Each participant also received a copy of the report.

Source: Judy Mosedale, Executive Director, Staunton Performing Arts Center, Staunton, VA. Phone (540) 885-3211.
E-mail: judy@stauntonperformingarts.org.
Website: www.stauntonperformingarts.org

Focus Group Questions Seek Community Input, Buy-in

Judy Mosedale, executive director, Staunton Performing Arts Center (Staunton, VA), shares eight main questions posed to four focus groups prior to launching a capital campaign to renovate and restore the Dixie Theatre:

1. What are your memories of the Dixie Theatre?

2. As the theatre is restored, what is it you think it should be for the community?

3. Should the board of directors retain the name, Dixie? Why or why not?

4. The theatre will become a presenting house, which means it will bring in entertainment from local productions to touring productions of all kinds, concerts, plays, musicals, children's productions, etc., as opposed to a producing house (a theatre that produces plays with an in-house repertory company, for example). What kind of performances/activities would you like to see at the theatre?

5. It has been estimated it will cost approximately $9.8 million to renovate/restore the theatre complex. Approximately $4.6 million will be needed from the community. Do you have suggestions on how best to raise these funds?

6. Do you know of groups (civic, youth, business) that might be interested in playing a role in the renovation/restoration of the theatre?

7. How do you suggest the community be kept informed as work progresses on the theatre?

8. What do you see as the greatest challenge the board will have to address as it renovates/restores the theatre?

Source: Judy Mosedale, Executive Director, Staunton Performing Arts Center, Staunton, VA. Phone (540) 885-3211.
E-mail: judy@stauntonperformingarts.org.
Website: www.stauntonperformingarts.org

Focus Group Brings Forth Nontraditional Case Statement

Instead of developing a one-time case statement to generate campaign support, officials with William Penn Charter School (Philadelphia, PA) developed a nontraditional case statement that told its message in a four-booklet series.

John Rogers, chief development officer, answers questions about the motivation for their recent nontraditional case statement and how it came to be:

"What sets your campaign's case statement apart from the rest?"

"Instead of rolling something out and then saying, 'What do you think of this?', our case statement was built upon language that was the result of a focus group of 24 of our school's stakeholders (e.g., students, teachers, alumni, parents and friends of the school)."

"What ideas were the result of the focus group?"

"One key phrase I remember that came from the conversations was the term 'counter-culture.' A participant said Penn Charter went against the culture in the way it educates its students. This phrase prompted us to ask: 'Why not do the same thing (go against the culture) in the way we market this?'"

"What is the purpose of each booklet?"

"Our campaign booklets are divided into four themes:
1) Are you part of Penn Charter's counter culture?
2) How do you define success?
3) What gives you hope?
4) Will you step out of line?
    Each booklet poses its question and ties specific stories

from alumni, teachers, parents and students reflective of Penn Charter."

"What made you take this risk with a nontraditional case statement?"

"We felt we had nothing to lose. We were at the point when the campaign had gone on so long (started in 1997-'98 and closed in June 2007), all major donors had weighed in and we still needed to raise $20 million. The books were the foundation for the public appeal and they paid off. We raised $15 million from our public appeal and more than $47 million for the entire campaign."

Source: John Rogers, Chief Development Officer, William Penn Charter School, Philadelphia, PA. Phone (215) 844-3460, ext. 111. E-mail: jarogers@penncharter.com

Content not available in this edition

How to Identify and Recruit Your Next Major Campaign Chair

Well-chosen chairs can make all the difference in a capital campaign's success. Just ask supporters of Junior Achievement of Central Indiana (Indianapolis, IN), where two influential community leaders were recently recruited to co-chair the final phase of a $5 million capital campaign.

> "Crack the door open.... That's the biggest thing campaign chairs can do for you."

Jeff Miller, president and CEO, speaks about the chairs' role:

"Why is it important to recruit the right campaign chair(s)?"

"There are six to eight campaigns going on in our community, so there is no lack of people asking for money. Having influential campaign chairs puts some significance on our campaign. It makes people think that it must be important or these guys wouldn't sign on to it.... Our chairmen — Bob Palmer, vice president of Air-Ground Freight Service-Central FedEx, and Gary Aletto, COO of Bright Sheet Metal and principle of GSA Investments — also have more influence with major donors, many of whom have also chaired campaigns and asked our chairmen to give to their campaigns.... Name recognition of community leaders is important, especially on a major campaign. We are in the last stages of a five-year campaign. We had different chairs for each phase. I am looking to our current chairmen to help me finish the job."

"What should you look for when enlisting a campaign chair?"

"Are they connected to the community you are raising funds from? Will their involvement cause others' involvement? Will they actually be of help to you? I plan on our co-chairs being extra feet on the ground for me, but primarily I need their help in opening doors. That's the biggest thing campaign chairs can do for you — crack the door open."

"How did you identify your campaign chairmen?"

"We were looking for people who had different audiences, who connected with the community in different ways, but were both well-known in their own right. We were also looking for people who had been very involved with our organization over the years — people who had a significant amount of time and money invested in our organization. By doing so, we have chairmen who are really speaking from the heart when out doing asks and promoting our campaign."

"How did you go about recruiting them to serve as co-chairmen?"

"It was a six-month process of looking at what we want to do, why and how. We were recruiting them as we were developing our strategy for the campaign. Because the conversation about chairing the campaign didn't happen the first time we spoke with them, but rather as an evolution of the process they were involved in, I would have been surprised if they had said no. When you recruit your campaign chairs as part of the campaign process ... you don't have to explain what you are trying to do because they should already know it backwards and forwards."

"What role will your co-chairmen play in your campaign?"

"They will go with me on about 25 percent of the asks. Their name will also be on all campaign letters. They recently assisted us on identifying our top 50 prospects."

Source: Jeff Miller, President and CEO, Junior Achievement of Central Indiana, Indianapolis, IN. Phone (317) 252-5900, ext. 202. E-mail: jeff@jaindy.org

Be Up Front About Chairperson's Expectations

Leading a capital campaign or major gifts committee demands can-do leadership. If your chairperson has a great reputation but no leadership skills, you'll get nowhere fast.

When planning a capital campaign or filling the top post on your major gifts committee, make sure your choice for chairperson clearly understands what's expected. Share a position description such as the sample at right during the recruitment process.

Draft a chairperson job description using the example shown here as a guide. Obviously the description of a campaign chair will differ from that of a major gifts committee chair, but the general focus is the same: to develop and follow through on a plan to generate many major gifts over time.

Major Gift Committee's Purpose

a. Identify and research new major gifts prospects (those capable of making outright and/or planned gifts of $25,000-plus).

b. Follow a relationship-building plan of cultivation that will move both prospects and past donors toward the realization of making major gifts.

c. Solicit major gifts as assigned.

d. Steward and appropriately recognize existing donors.

Committee Chairperson Responsibilities

1. Work to identify and recruit committee members with capacity to identify, cultivate, solicit and steward major gift donors.

2. Work with staff in the development of an ongoing board and volunteer-driven major gifts plan.

3. Assist in educating and motivating committee members in their responsibilities.

4. Call and conduct regular meetings with committee members.

5. Set example for all committee members in terms of personal giving and contacts with donors and would-be donors.

6. To represent the committee to the board of trustees and at other public functions as necessary.

Don't Accept Just Anyone to Chair Your Campaign

Do you hold a community-wide campaign each year? Does it include a handpicked chairperson who can lead the way and inspire others? Before naming just anyone who is willing to be labeled campaign chair, give some thought to who would make the ideal leader for your effort. The person you select should:

1. Have a history of commitment to your organization in terms of both generous support and involvement.
2. Be known and respected among a majority of those you plan to solicit.
3. Possess a track record of leadership and dependability for taking on a job and living up to its demands.

Appoint an Honorary Chair to Your Capital Campaign

Lake Forest College (Lake Forest, IL) is in the midst of a $100 million capital campaign. Among those leading the campaign is an honorary chairperson.

"Including an honorary chair in your capital campaign provides a wonderful opportunity to recognize and involve a key supporter ... who may not be able to provide the day-to-day volunteer leadership for a capital campaign," says Pam Gerard, vice president, development and alumni relations. Additionally, "It demonstrates to your constituents that this important person believes in the vitality of your organization and its future."

Often, this simple demonstration of support, combined with an ask, encourages others to give generously, Gerard says.

"Our honorary chair is a life trustee of the college," she says. "When our trustees were being solicited in the early phase of the campaign, he often spoke passionately at board meetings about the importance of giving at a leadership level, and he also assisted with several solicitations. His involvement helped us to meet our trustee giving goals."

When seeking an honorary chair, Gerard recommends searching for a person who:

- Is committed to your organization's history, as well as its future.

- Shows unwavering leadership and can motivate others.

- Provides strong financial support.

- Is willing to help cultivate and solicit key prospects.

- Is well-recognized in your community and able to be an ambassador for your cause.

When your organization identifies the right individual to serve as honorary chair, Gerard says, "Your campaign will have a key person who can advocate on behalf of the institution and can inspire others to offer their support."

Source: Pam Gerard, Vice President, Development and Alumni Relations, Lake Forest College, Lake Forest, IL. Phone (847) 735-6003. E-mail: gerard@lakeforest.edu

Establish and Share Steering Committee Duties

To help your campaign steering committee set a successful course, be sure all members receive and review a job description that includes the following key duties:

- ✓ To make a personal campaign commitment that sets the bar for gifts that follow.

- ✓ To provide general direction and active management of the campaign.

- ✓ To establish goals and quotas.

- ✓ To set the operating schedule for the campaign.

- ✓ To recruit and coordinate activities of volunteers.

- ✓ To participate in leadership calls.

- ✓ To monitor campaign progress and make necessary adjustments.

How to Harness the Power of Volunteers, Board Members in Fund Development

COMMUNICATING WITH BOARD MEMBERS AND VOLUNTEERS

Communication with your volunteers and board members should be: regular but at irregular intervals; ongoing but not constant; appropriate but not contrived; customized but not canned; and planned, but should seem unplanned. The practice of relationship building with a volunteer is not unlike that of a would-be donor. Use a variety of communication approaches to stay connected with both volunteers and board members: group settings, one-on-one meetings, print, e-mail, personal correspondence, phone and more.

Assemble a Top-notch Toolkit to Boost Volunteer Involvement

Fundraising toolkits should empower and enthuse volunteers, making them feel they have all they need to represent your nonprofit accurately and assuredly.

For inspiration on assembling your fundraising toolkit, look inside one from Friends of Amani U.S. (Rockland, MA), a nonprofit that conducts volunteer fundraising on behalf of Amani, a refuge for homeless children founded in Tanzania in 2001. Because Amani is based in Africa, its fundraising toolkit needs to accomplish the task of fully educating its American volunteers, even if they've never visited Amani in person.

The organization's toolkit for volunteer fundraisers contains:

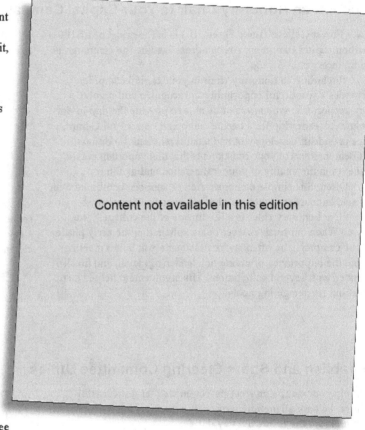

Content not available in this edition

✓ A thank-you letter addressed to its volunteers on the very first page (shown at right).

✓ A Five Minutes or Less list bulleting the most important facts Amani fundraisers should convey to potential donors even if they don't have much time to spend with them. Val McDyer, president of Friends of Amani U.S., says that being able to "quote facts in support of our fundraising" is a critical component of their success.

✓ Specific statistics. For example, the Amani toolkit notes that "Thirty-eight percent of (Tanzanian) children are moderately or severely stunted for their age, implying significant chronic malnutrition." Immediately following this fact, the toolkit states that "The children at Amani receive three nutritious meals a day."

✓ An Every Donation Counts list that shows how a $100 gift buys 25 textbooks, $250 buys 33 pairs of shoes and so on. Lisa Anderson, a chairperson of the Parent-Teacher Organization at Three Oaks Elementary (Cary, IL), says this information helped her school raise funds on behalf of Amani. "I felt that if (the students) understood what they were bringing their coins in for that it would be more successful."

✓ First-person testimonials from American volunteers working with Amani in Africa and biographies of children who live at Amani. McDyer supplements these with information on the role Friends of Amani plays in fundraising to reassure donors they are donating to a reputable nonprofit and that their money will be well handled.

✓ Easy how-tos for planning fundraising events from pancake breakfasts to movie marathons, board game tournaments, even a head-shaving special event.

✓ A list of other helpful materials fundraisers can request: photos of the children, videos and CDs, Tanzanian fabric and art, drawings by the Amani children, etc. Anderson says this element helped connect students to the cause. "It was fun for them to see that Amani children liked to draw with markers, pastels and crayons just like them!"

✓ Pre-formatted sign-up and sponsorship sheets for all kinds of fundraising events.

✓ Another thank-you letter at the end.

Source: Val McDyer, President, Friends of Amani U.S., Rockland, MA. Phone (617) 521-8335. E-mail: VMcDyer@yahoo.com. Website: www.friendsofamani.com

Handout Offers Ways to Help

How proactive are you at encouraging all existing donors to help, in whatever ways they choose, with major gifts? Why not create a user-friendly handout you can leave with donors that illustrates the many ways they can help your major gifts efforts?

It makes good sense to invite all current donors to serve as centers of influence in whatever capacity they choose. Some will obviously be more helpful and involved than others. Those who become more active will deserve more of your attention. Those who choose to do little or nothing will at least be more aware of the need for additional support.

Also, those donors who elect to assist will become even more committed to your cause by virtue of their increased involvement.

Below is a generic handout you can use as a template in creating one tailored to your own circumstances.

We Invite You to Serve as an Ambassador for XYZ Nonprofit

You have already proven your belief in XYZ Nonprofit and its mission by virtue of your generous support. And for that we are deeply grateful.

But we would be remiss if we didn't extend an invitation for you to help us identify and nurture relationships with others who might one day make similar gifts.

We invite you to serve as an Ambassador of XYZ Nonprofit in whatever capacity you choose: identifying those capable of making significant gifts ($25,000 or more), helping make introductions, nurturing relationships and more.

Please review the many ways you can help and then contact any member of the Advancement Team to discuss those options in more detail.

We welcome your involvement!

Ways you can help —

Donor Identification

Name	Relationship	Contact Info

Research
____ Sharing background information
____ Rating and screening potential donors
____ Sharing news clippings
____ Sharing other charities' lists of contributors
____ Serving on a committee
____ Other _____

Relationship Building
____ Making introductions
____ Hosting a get-acquainted event (home, place of business, etc.)
____ Accompanying a staff member on a cultivation call
____ Serving on a committee
____ Other _____

Soliciting a Gift
____ Accompanying a staff member on a solicitation call
____ Serving on a committee
____ Other _____

Stewardship
____ Writing a letter of appreciation to an existing donor
____ Making a thank-you call on a current donor
____ Other _____
_____

Your Name _____ E-mail _____
Daytime Phone _____ Evening Phone _____

Offer Online Volunteer Sign-up

Want to do more to encourage individuals to get involved in fund development — in any capacity that works for them? Why not list fund development opportunities on your website and include an online sign-up form?

Offering several types of volunteer opportunities: 1) results in greater volunteer involvement, 2) allows your office to accomplish more, and 3) makes the public more aware of the many ways in which they can take part in the life of your organization and its work.

Come up with an online checklist of volunteer opportunities related to various aspects of fund development. Then set up your site to allow visitors to complete an online volunteer form, or at least to e-mail your office and indicate their interest areas.

ZYZ Medical Center
Anywhere U.S.A.

*We could sure
use some help!*

Tom: Is there any chance you could help us by making a few phone calls at our upcoming Phonathon — October 15-21, from 5:30 to 9:00 pm? Call me (232-0433) or sign up online. Thanks!

Molly

To offer your assistance — whether it's an hour or a day or on an ongoing basis — please sign up on our website: www.zyzmedcenter.com

---

You might even take it a step further and drive would-be volunteers to your website. Develop a postcard (such as the one shown here) that can be sent to individuals, asking them to volunteer for a particular project, then encouraging them to visit your website to sign up online.

Increase Board Productivity With a Dedicated Intranet

To increase the efficiency and effectiveness of board members, staff and volunteers, streamline information and resource sharing with a dedicated organizational intranet.

The intranet at the San Diego Asian Film Foundation (SDAFF), San Diego, CA, "is a private online space where stakeholders can find everything from time cards to information on current and prospective grants," says Lee Ann Kim, executive director.

Using unique user names and passwords, board members use the intranet to find staff contact information, detailed biographies of other board members, meeting schedules, calendars and key financial information, along with connecting board membership with sponsorship records.

"Savvy fundraisers can click on any of the 500 or so sponsors that have supported us over the last 12 years and see their history of giving, any recent interactions with us, and a current name and contact number," says Kim. "They never have to wonder if this or that company is on board with a project."

She says the system, custom built for the foundation in 2002, was revolutionary for its time. But while it still offers many advantages, Kim says applications like Google docs have come to approximate many of its functions.

Source: Lee Ann Kim, Executive Director, San Diego Asian Film Foundation, San Diego, CA. Phone (858) 565-1264. E-mail: Leeann@sdaff.org. Website: http://www.sdaff.org

Meet One-on-one With Board Members

From a development standpoint, regularly meeting one on one with your board members makes sense.

In the face-to-face sessions, you can:

✓ Review fiscal year giving to date.

✓ Talk key issues/challenges at hand.

✓ Brainstorm about whom to approach for a challenge gift.

✓ Identify their associates/friends who might merit a personal visit.

✓ Address funding interests of individual board members.

✓ Come up with new ways to address your nonprofit's strategic plans from a fundraising standpoint.

✓ Toss around ways in which the board can positively participate in and impact development events/programs, especially major and planned gifts.

Expand Your Volunteer Base

Once your year is planned and you have key dates for the development shop in writing — receptions, special events, phonathon — send an e-mail or letter to constituents pointing out volunteer involvement opportunities. Include a return response mechanism.

Keep Development Committee Members Up-to-date

It's nice to get a thank-you letter from a charity employee. But it's much more powerful and meaningful to receive a letter from a board member or volunteer — someone who's not getting paid to say thank you.

Whenever your development committee meets, include current information about donors and prospects that members can act on if they choose. Whether it's a handwritten note for a recent gift or a birthday card, the added touch of these devoted individuals will only serve to strengthen your organization's ties to both donors and prospects.

Items you may wish to make development committee members aware of include:

✓ Recent contributions of previous and new donors.
✓ Upcoming special dates of donors: birthdays, anniversaries, etc.
✓ Job promotions and other news items related to donors and prospects.

Give your committee members some stationery and note cards with your organization's letterhead so the recipient of the card or letter will make an immediate connection with your organization.

Breakfast With a Board Member

Looking for a way to involve board members or development committee members in the cultivation and solicitation of gifts? Launch a breakfast with a board member program:

1. At your next meeting, share with your board or development committee a list of persons representing noncontributing businesses. Explain that you want to have breakfast with each board member individually sometime during the next 60 days. (It will be up to each board member to contact you to set up a time that works.)

2. Instruct the board that each member is to invite one individual on the list to join the two of you for breakfast.

The board member is to clear the name of the prospect he/she intends to invite in advance to be sure that name has not been taken.

3. The board member then invites the prospect to join the two of you for breakfast.

4. Use the breakfast meeting to introduce your cause and establish rapport or, if the prospect is well aware of your organization and its programs, to solicit a gift. You and the board member will need to visit before the get-together to decide the objective of the meeting.

Confirm Volunteer Assignments in Writing

When working with a campaign steering committee, board development committee or other volunteers involved in cultivating and soliciting major gifts, spell out expectations.

When a meeting includes individual assignments, follow up with a memo to each volunteer that confirms what's expected of them and deadlines. Having assignments in writing emphasizes the importance of follow up and reflects a higher level of professionalism on your part.

Below is a generic follow-up assignment memo to use as a template:

Memo   ROLLAND ACADEMY

R_A

To: Mark Anderson
From: Davis Winberg
RE: Follow-up Assignments
Date: January 15, 2010

Based on our most recent meeting, your call assignments include the following:

Prospect	Action	Deadline
Baron Consulting	Cultivation: Determine funding interest	2/12/10
Margaret Mason	Solicitation w/President	2/12/10
M/M M Hansen	Submit proposal; set follow up date	2/12/10
Andrew Miller	Solicit naming gift w/Bartley	2/12/10
Susan Hanes	Introductory call w/Bartley	2/12/10

If you have any questions or need any assistance, please contact Mary Prentler at 555-2984. As always, it's important that everyone complete their assigned calls on time to complete our list as planned.

What Should You Report to Your Board and Volunteers?

Campaign progress reporting is a powerful tool for both fundraising professionals and an organization's professional staff and volunteer leadership, says Roy P. Wheeler, Jr., executive vice president, Custom Development Solutions (New York, NY).

It is important to quickly and effectively set the pace and tone for campaign communications and monitoring at the beginning of the campaign, Wheeler says. Doing so helps make the effort a success while allowing issues to be addressed early on, helping to foster the best working relationship among staff, board and volunteers.

The major gift officer or consultant is responsible for establishing immediate and clear lines of communication with top professional staff and volunteer leadership (directors or trustees), especially within current development operations, Wheeler says. "This eases accomplishment of the tasks required during the course of the campaign, and facilitates everyone's understanding of what is happening, and who is responsible for making it happen. The progress report is the primary tool in this strategy."

He establishes report cycles up front, as well as who should be reported to, then creates a first report that outlines each major campaign activity. He presents this report in a special meeting, first with the top development professional, then with the chief professional officer of the organization.

Once Wheeler has buy-in of these key persons, he schedules a meeting to present the report to his volunteer leaders.

Lastly, he presents a formal copy of the report to the organization's board as an agenda item at a regular board meeting.

When making a report, Wheeler says, "You need to take into account that there will be some crossover as a campaign builds a parallel leadership team focused on the campaign, but that typically includes key board members and professional staff."

Source: Roy P. Wheeler, Jr., Executive Vice President, Custom Development Solutions, Inc., New York, NY. Phone (800) 761-3833. E-mail: rpw@cdsfunds.com

---

Essential Elements of a Campaign Progress Report

Campaign progress reports should include certain specific elements, says Roy P. Wheeler, Jr., executive vice president, Custom Development Solutions (New York, NY).

Those elements include:

- **Statistical summary of overall campaign status,** including funds raised in relation to goal, number of gift requests made, number of decisions received (yeses and nos), commitments received, percent of participation (number of yeses to decisions), average gift and time left in campaign timetable.

- **General narrative summary of what's happening in the campaign during that report period,** and where the campaign is in relation to the timetable and expectations.

- **Specific summary of ongoing phases of activity** including relevant statistics, assignments, upcoming activities, actions required, etc.

- **Logistical update:** e.g., budget, expenses, issues requiring attention, status of materials development.

- **Statement regarding pledge redemption activities,** whether they are on course and if relevant issues need attention.

- **Specific list of priority action items** for upcoming report period.

How to Harness the Power of Volunteers, Board Members in Fund Development

For them to be effective and stay motivated, volunteers require your ongoing attention. Make expectations clear by having job and committee descriptions. Follow up assignments in writing. Provide volunteers with adequate training and ongoing education. And never forget to recognize volunteers' accomplishments, both individually and publicly.

Job Description Adds Substance to Centers of Influence Appointees

To broaden your organization's visibility and fund-raising success geographically, work to establish centers of influence — volunteer ambassadors who work on behalf of your cause — in communities, counties and/or regions.

Having volunteers work on your behalf regionally will help your fund development efforts multiply throughout a large geographic area.

But before you begin to assemble clusters of centers of influence willing to work on your behalf, take the time to outline the intended scope of the ambassadors' responsibilities by producing a job description like the one shown here.

A written job description will accomplish two important objectives: 1) It will help to better convey just what is expected of those who consider assisting your organization, and 2) It will help you to more clearly decide just what it is you want these willing individuals to do for you. A written job description will give meaning to the position and also enable you to establish more clearcut expectations of what each volunteer is to do.

If you're just getting started with a centers of influence program, you may even want to include your first recruits in shaping the job description. If your top volunteers have a say in what's expected of others, they will more fully own the program and want it to succeed as much as you do.

Be sure to include a beginning and ending date for your volunteers. This may make them more willing to accept a position — since they know it's for a defined period of time — and there's nothing to keep you from reappointing those volunteers who are enthusiastic and dedicated to your cause. Likewise, this allows you to end the working relationship with those who are less than enthusiastic about becoming involved in the effort. They can simply receive a letter of thanks at the conclusion of their first year.

Build your core of regional volunteers by establishing a centers of influence program and using a job description during the recruitment process. You'll find it to be a worthwhile use of your time.

Develop a job description you can use to establish expectations for regional centers of influence.

CENTERS OF INFLUENCE
JOB DESCRIPTION

Centers of influence include those persons who agree to serve as official ambassadors on behalf of [Name of Organization] for a period of one year.

Members of this elite group agree to represent [Name of Organization] in their respective communities and to build support for [Name of Organization].

Responsibilities include, but are not limited to:

- ❑ Identifying individuals, businesses, foundations, etc. in your community/region who have the financial ability to support [Name of Organization] in a generous way — through outright and/or planned gifts.

- ❑ Cultivating positive relationships with members of your community/region on behalf of [Name of Organization].

- ❑ Offering advice and sharing your citizens' perceptions regarding [Name of Organization].

- ❑ Bringing members of your community/region as guests to events hosted by [Name of Organization].

- ❑ Identifying and enlisting other centers of influence willing to serve as ambassadors on behalf of [Name of Organization].

- ❑ Soliciting gifts on behalf of [Name of Organization] when appropriate.

- ❑ Thanking past donors for their contributions.

- ❑ Establishing positive rapport with your community's agents of wealth (e.g., attorneys, accountants, trust officers).

I agree to represent [Name of Organization] as an official center of influence for the community/region of:

_____

beginning _____ through _____

_____   _____
Signature   Signature
Center of Influence   Executive Director

How to Work With a High-powered Volunteer

One of your community's most valued leaders — the CEO of a Fortune 500 company, one of your region's most wealthy individuals or someone of like nature — has agreed to lend his/her name to your fundraising campaign, and offer assistance to you. Knowing this person has a schedule packed with business obligations, travel, family and other commitments, how can you accommodate the high-powered tycoon so he/she will find working with you a pleasant (and ongoing) experience?

- **Ask which friends or business associates you may contact.** Your high-powered supporter will have dozens of other influential contacts that he/she may urge you to approach. But avoid assuming who those might be, and ask for ideas or a list of appropriate names. Also ask if you may use his/her name when you connect, as in, "Mr. Peterson suggested that I visit with you about our campaign."

- **Identify what the person most enjoys doing.** Maybe your donor isn't a telephone-oriented type, but loves greeting guests and mingling at events. Is he/she a good public speaker who would enjoy being at your kickoff meeting, or a better letter writer? Cater to those desires whenever possible, allowing him/her to choose how he/she will be most visible and vocal in support of your charity.

- **Arrange one or two media interviews.** Many highly successful persons are reluctant to be interviewed about their business accomplishments or wealth, but will be accommodating if the news angle is about support of a good cause. Ask in advance which type of coverage you may arrange, and even which reporter to call if possible. Depending on the name recognition of your supporter, some news organizations are pleased to have any opportunity to interview or photograph such high-powered persons.

- **Be understanding and prepared to react to unexpected schedule conflicts.** If your valued supporter must cancel a meeting or appearance due to business or other reason, have a backup plan ready. The influential person will have all the same routine schedule juggling that you have, plus a higher probability of business situations interfering. When conflicts arise, try to reschedule as soon as possible or cancel altogether.

- **Consider the executive assistant as your primary contact.** Chances are you will speak a great deal more often to his or her assistant or secretary (that's what they're for). Be patient when you find it difficult to talk to the chief personally. The assistant can brief him/her on any of your questions or concerns, then call you back with an answer or a solution.

- **Obtain a photograph, signature and company letterhead at your first meeting.** If you have permission to use them, arrange to obtain them up front. Send photographs of the person attached to news releases, and use his/her signature on appeal letters. Since there is rarely a need to ask for these items more than once, keep using what you have as long as possible.

- **Send copies of all letters, news releases and publications in advance.** Even if you have been given latitude in your use of the person's name and photograph, fax a copy of each item to the office a few days in advance of use. Call the assistant to confirm receipt. Keep the possibility for after-the-fact objections to a minimum. You are not being a pest, but keeping them updated.

- **Thank your giant volunteer in meaningful ways.** By this time, you have developed a solid connection with people who are close to your supporter. Ask them for insight into heartfelt ways you may thank him/her for his/her tremendous help. If the consensus is that a simple note is sufficient, follow that advice.

Get Off to a Good Beginning

As you work to establish a working relationship with your volunteer of prominence, keep in mind that time is money — for both of you — by using some of these guidelines:

1. Develop a time line of when you must meet.

2. Remember that you will be doing the majority of the work, and that input from your valued contact need not be extensive or time-consuming.

3. Work with his/her executive assistant to choose two or three brief times for personal meetings.

4. Be highly organized when these meetings take place, ideally for no more than 20 minutes.

5. Keep your remarks or questions to about five minutes, leaving more time for his/her ideas or input.

Monitor Key Contributions of Your Centers of Influence

If you currently involve board members and other volunteers as centers of influence — those actively involved in fund development on your behalf — or intend to do so in the near future, then it's important to give them the attention they deserve. Their success will have a direct correlation to the amount of training and support received along the way.

If you expect centers of influence to produce results, then it's important to make them fully aware of those expectations and that their progress is being monitored.

Whether these volunteers meet monthly or quarterly, make use of a form such as the example below to point out the degree to which participants are meeting agreed-to objectives. Such a form demonstrates the seriousness of volunteers' efforts and also serves as a subtle way to recognize achievers and admonish under-performers.

Know that whatever criteria you choose to track throughout the year will become the primary focus of your volunteers' efforts since that is how they are being judged.

CENTERS OF INFLUENCE QUARTERLY STATUS REPORT *December 31, 2009*					
Centers of Influence	Contributed Hours	Hosted Events	New Introductions	Solicited Gifts New/Renewed	Amount Raised New/Renewed
M Leon	68	3	41	17/8	$ 4,000/9,500
S Knight	27	2	19	9/3	$ 950/1,550
R Mahony	31	1	17	10/10	$ 2,100/6,750
J Pinney	80	4	56	30/17	$ 8,400/9,900
S Stiffel	17	—	8	2/8	$ 660/9,500
L Albert	34	1	22	11/5	$ 3,000/1,500
M Rubin	31	1	20	8/12	$ 2,250/7,000
B Morgan	15	1	17	12/3	$ 2,800/2,500
C Hadden	19	1	21	11/8	$ 3,200/9,000
C Fiedler	66	3	45	29/14	$ 9,500/9,800
R Sliefert	81	5	67	45/19	$15,850/12,000
TOTAL	469	22	333	184/107	$52,710/78,950

Volunteer Managers Assuming More Responsibility in Development Shops

A growing trend is taking place in America: Increasing numbers of nonprofit organizations are creating volunteer manager positions to assist in involving and engaging increased numbers of people in various aspects of their nonprofits' work.

Why? To broaden their donor bases.

It's a well-proven fact that increased involvement eventually results in financial support as well. By charging one individual with managing volunteer involvement, you can encourage and track a much higher level of volunteer participation. Even though many employees may be encouraged to make greater use of volunteers, the volunteer manager can serve as the advocate and support system for other employees who work to involve volunteers.

Hospitals have traditionally taken the lead in hiring professional volunteer managers to recruit, nurture and engage volunteers, but this movement is now taking hold with many other types of nonprofit organizations as well. The individual's title may vary among nonprofit types, but the aim is the same — to enlist, cultivate and manage increasing numbers of volunteers.

Whether you add the responsibility of volunteer manager to

Director of Volunteer Services
Position Description Goals for 2010
- To increase the number of active volunteers to [X] throughout the current fiscal year.
- To manage and monitor all volunteer actions/involvement.
- To serve as a volunteer advocate and support system for all other employees.
- To work with employees in identifying opportunities for volunteer involvement.
- To implement a training and recognition system for all volunteers.
- To annually evaluate all volunteer-related programs.

an existing position or hire someone who is specifically charged with the responsibility, give serious thought to adding this set of responsibilities to your development efforts if your long-term goal is to expand your number of financial contributors over time.

Deal With Deadbeat Volunteers

Any development shop that involves volunteers has them: a handful of persons who readily agree to sign up for projects but fail to show up or complete tasks.

Here are eight ideas to help you improve such volunteers' track records:

1. **Enlist help from steadfast volunteers.** Since they carry the heaviest share of the load for no-shows, they may be eager to call their neglectful counterparts and suggest a leave of absence from the project until their schedules permit greater involvement.

2. **Provide complete descriptions for volunteer jobs.** Review requirements before arriving at a mutual agreement in a businesslike approach that implies they are assuming an important assignment.

3. **Adopt a point system of completed volunteer hours (or tasks) with incentives.** Tracking time spent and tasks completed both recognizes the doers while allowing the less committed to see the disparity of involvement in concrete terms.

4. **Offer no-shows a graceful escape route.** Let them know you've noticed their apparent conflict each time they have pledged to assist. Ask if you can help in any way. If behavior doesn't change, let them off the hook by allowing them to resign.

5. **Stop encouraging their participation.** Subtly recategorize the vanishing volunteer as a supporting member of the project. Instead of asking for time, request an underwriting gift.

6. **Assign a tactful watchdog to certain volunteers.** Many unenthused volunteers simply need someone to be there to ignite them, offer encouragement, spell out what needs to be done and share sufficient excitement about the project.

7. **Develop a list of lower priority tasks.** Every organization has counterproductive volunteers who won't show up to help, yet refuse to let go. Establish a list of tasks for them that, if completed, will enhance the project but, if not, will not impede productive volunteers' efforts.

8. **Encourage a mentor approach between veteran and new volunteers.**

Form Provides Helpful Way to Monitor Activity

All too often, procrastination and other distractions prevent development personnel from carrying out those functions that are most critical — making regular contact with prospects and donors.

Recording that activity weekly helps to reinforce its importance among all involved.

If you manage others who are responsible for calling on prospects and donors as a part of their responsibilities, it's important to have them regularly record their activity.

Why? For several reasons. First, doing so helps them more accurately analyze how their time is being spent. Secondly, it helps you, as the manager, to monitor how their time is being used. And finally, the written report provides a lasting record that can be used to improve effectiveness as you plan subsequent years' goals and objectives.

Whether staff track cultivation and solicitation activity via computer software, their PDA or with a simple pen and notebook, the report should include the kinds of information provided on the weekly calls report depicted below.

Content not available in this edition

How to Harness the Power of Volunteers, Board Members in Fund Development

SHOWING APPRECIATION AND RECOGNITION TO VOLUNTEERS AND BOARD MEMBERS

The best way to retain accomplished volunteers is by acknowledging them whenever they come through for you. Doesn't matter whether their achievement is large or small. Your affirmation tells them you're aware of their contributions and appreciate them. They need to know that. That's what will keep them coming back for more. That's what will encourage them to be true ambassadors for your organization and attract other volunteers in the process.

Recognize Fund Development Volunteers

To build your base of volunteers involved with various aspects of fund development, why not start an annual awards program that recognizes these special volunteers? Here's a list of the types of awards you might consider:

Rookie of the Year Award — Given to the newest volunteer who rose to the occasion and set an example for others.

Distinguished Volunteer of the Year — Awarded to someone who has been involved with fund development over a period of years and/or made a significant difference in your fundraising efforts.

Ambassador of the Year — Awarded to that individual who was out spreading the good news about your charity to everyone with whom they came in contact.

Hidden Gem Award — Given to that individual who worked tirelessly behind the scenes (e.g., researching, writing, making phone calls) to help your fundraising efforts.

Leadership Award — Presented to the volunteer who did the most to rally other volunteers in various aspects of fund development.

Feature Volunteer Leadership

Never miss an opportunity to include your top volunteer leadership in any public announcements related to fundraising projects: annual campaign kickoffs, capital campaign announcements, ground-breaking ceremonies and more. Here are three key reasons for doing this:

1. Public announcements serve to further connect your leadership to the project.
2. Your volunteer leaders will assume greater ownership of the project.
3. The public will associate those volunteer leaders with your agency.

Give Volunteers Equal Billing

Do you publish and distribute an annual honor roll of donors? What about volunteers? Are they prominently listed alongside your donors? Be sure any published donor lists also include the names of those who have given their time.

Showcase Your Top Volunteer Solicitors

Whenever you're fortunate enough to have a volunteer who takes the initiative to raise funds for your organization with little help on your part, publicize those efforts — as long as the volunteer agrees to go along with it. Why? Two reasons:

1. Volunteers who enthusiastically solicit gifts on their own are a rare breed and deserve all the recognition you're willing to give them.
2. Showcasing successful volunteer solicitors works wonders in encouraging others to do the same.

Tout Campaign Leadership

Don't miss any opportunities to publicly display and recognize the many able leaders involved in your campaign.

Officials with The University of Pennsylvania include a Leadership tab on their website that lists all individuals involved as volunteers.

Leadership categories include: a) chair and co-chairs, b) steering committee and c) major gift committee. In all, 125 volunteer names are listed. Now that's involvement!

Unique Ways to Thank Your Campaign Steering Committee

At the end of your multi-year capital campaign, thank members of your campaign steering committee or other key players with a thoughtful gift such as:

A Personalized Symbolic Award: Therese O'Malley, director of benefactor relations, Northwestern Memorial Foundation (Chicago, IL), says at the end of a seven-year campaign that raised $206.4 million against a $150 million goal, they presented steering committee members with a custom-made crystal pyramid award engraved with the campaign total, a message of gratitude and the member's name. "Like many other fundraising shops, we used the campaign pyramid to track our fundraising success throughout the campaign," O'Malley says. "As this became a symbol of our progress, it seemed to be an appropriate item to honor our campaign steering committee members for their years of hard work."

Meaningful Framed Photographs: Kay Coughlin, director of stewardship, Oberlin College (Oberlin, OH), has worked with Memorable Miniatures, Akron, OH, to produce miniature portraits of campus buildings. The portraits include a message on back that in part reads: "….recognizing Oberlin's most generous philanthropists."

"The execution of these portraits is excellent and the production quality is quite high," Coughlin says. "It is a great value for the dollar. We have used these for our largest donors and they are a hit."

Handcrafted Artwork: Doug Draut, director of leadership gifts, Centre College (Danville, KY), says they utilize the internationally known glass artist/instructor of their glass-blowing program to create unique pieces for each campaign executive committee member. "These were very well received and are collector's items," he says. "It made the 'thank you' very distinctive and exclusive."

*Sources: Therese O'Malley, Director, Benefactor Relations, Northwestern Memorial Foundation, Chicago, IL. Phone (312) 926-2466. E-mail: thomalle@nmh.org
Kay Coughlin, Director of Stewardship, Oberlin College, Oberlin, OH. Phone (440) 775-8569. E-mail: Kay.Coughlin@oberlin.edu
Doug Draut, Director of Leadership Gifts, Centre College, Danville, KY. Phone (877) 678-9822. E-mail: doug.draut@centre.edu*

How to Harness the Power of Volunteers, Board Members in Fund Development

MORE EXAMPLES OF HOW TO INVOLVE VOLUNTEERS, BOARD MEMBERS IN FUND DEVELOPMENT

Looking for more ways of involving and engaging volunteers and board members in fund development? Check out these additional ways of reaching out.

Eight Tips to Help Facilitate Successful Focus Groups

Focus groups — structured group interviews of six to 10 persons in which a facilitator asks open-ended questions to keep discussion on track — can be a great way to gain input from certain groups.

Ken Steele, senior vice president, education marketing, Academica Group, Inc. (London, Ontario, Canada), shares eight tips for facilitating successful focus groups:

1. Verify findings with multiple focus groups, in different geographies, different times of day, and with selected segments. Don't hang any key decisions on one or two focus groups; a single personality could dominate a group and create odd results.

2. Segment participants depending on purpose of your groups. Selection of participants is the first, vital step; think carefully about the criteria.

3. Set the stage early for open input, confidentiality, respect and taking turns, but stick to an agenda to keep on task.

4. Ensure the facilitator moves from general to specific, takes notes of private thoughts, and includes variety and fun.

5. Be patient. Be comfortable with dead air, as sometimes the best comments come after a few moments or even a minute of silence.

6. Find concrete tasks, issues, photos or problems to focus their attention. Get them to talk about personal experiences, not theorize broadly about causes and effects. You don't want amateur marketers; you want to know their own feelings and experiences.

7. Focus objectives on four or fewer key questions. Summarize that focus at the top of recruitment notes, discussion guide and post-focus group report. Go beyond the nice-to-knows to cover the need-to-knows.

8. Remember a focus group is a qualitative research experience, not quantitative methodology. "What you can get from focus groups are great new ideas, insights into how some people feel, what some people think and how some people react."

Source: Ken Steele, Senior Vice President, Education Marketing, Academica Group, London, Ontario, Canada. Phone (866) 922-8636. E-mail: ken@academicagroup.com

Donor Testimonials Speak Volumes

Successfully utilizing donor testimonials on your organization's website can encourage donations and make a statement about your organization.

"Testimonials not only inspire additional gifts, they are a form of donor recognition that shows the organization isn't interested in just the bottom dollar, it is interested in what the donor finds meaningful," says Tina Thome, director, The Ohio State University's Campus Campaign.

Thome offers advice for including donor testimonials on your website:

- **Keep testimonials short and meaningful.** While ease in making a gift is a great testimonial, the stories behind the gifts are what resonates with prospective donors.

- **Include testimonials from all giving levels and types.** "Whether gifts are large or small, they represent what the donor believes in or is passionate about, and that is what the testimonials tell the reader and inspires gifts," she says.

- **Capture the donor's uniqueness** while emphasizing the commonality of the cause.

- **Determine how to identify donors.** For instance, would they rather you use their full name or their initials and hometown? Or, would they rather remain anonymous?

- **Limit the number and rotate the testimonials on your website.** "Different elements speak to different donors," Thome says. "That is why having a variety of testimonials available is essential."

Source: Tina Thome, Director, Campus Campaign, The Ohio State University, Office of University Development, Columbus, OH. Phone (614) 292-3065. E-mail: thome.3@osu.edu. Website: www.osu.edu

Do You Have a Guest Experts Program in Place?

Here's an idea that nearly any type of nonprofit can adapt to cultivate relationships with major gift prospects: create a guest experts program as a way to engage individuals in the life and work of your organization. Your experts could be business executives, artists, scholars, celebrities, teachers, consultants or others.

A guest experts program not only cultivates a relationship with would-be donors, it can help build relationships with those who benefit from the guest expert's insight.

To establish a guest experts program (or strengthen an existing program), keep these points in mind:

Timing —

- Make sure the schedule works for your guest, allowing flexibility for additional time with the audience if needed.
- Schedule sessions with the expert around other events. Tie them in thematically, or draw on the added exposure to boost attendance.

Audience —

- Define your group based on what you want to accomplish with the event.
- You may want to limit the session to select groups (e.g., special guests, donors, board members) to add an element of exclusivity and interaction with the expert.
- Inviting large groups can also be beneficial, especially if sessions are styled in a lecture format. This broadens the range of exposure for your organization.
- Some sessions are more successful when they are open to the public, especially if fees can be charged to the attendees. This format focuses more on cultivating the guest expert rather than the audience.

Marketing the Event —

- The formats you choose to promote the event will depend on the audience you plan to reach. In-house publications and direct mail work best for smaller groups while tradi-

tional media outlets, such as news releases, will get your message to a larger, more diverse population.
- Make sure your brochures and programs reflect the event's quality and prestige.

Selecting the Experts —

- Guests should be experts in their fields and known by those you hope to draw.
- They should be respected by their peers. If they only have niche recognition, market to that select group.
- The most important aspect of guest experts is their ability to impart knowledge that is fulfilling to everyone involved, including the guest. Prepare guests so they know what type of audience they will have and what will be expected of them.

Cultivation —

- If the experience is successful for the expert and attendees, the event can serve as a cultivation tool for both groups. Follow-up visits to the expert should include discussions about the impact of his/her presentation.
- These events can generate a variety of gifts such as funds to help cover future guest expert programs, grants from the expert's company, original works of art from artists, royalties from books and patents, and more.
- Except for attendance revenues, separate the solicitation process from the event. The presentation serves to cultivate a relationship which later leads to a gift.

Annual Program —

- If an event with a certain expert is successful, consider making it an annual event.
- Be on the lookout for future experts within and outside your donor constituency.
- Keep the quality level high, and establish it as a prestigious honor. This will help with the cultivation aspect of the process.

Get a Letter-writing Campaign Underway

Want to broaden your base of donors? Round up a group of existing donors who would be willing to send solicitation letters to their friends, relatives and associates.

Assemble your group to share several types of solicitation letters they can use as guides in preparing their own letters. Give them the option of preparing and sending their own letters or having your office prepare them for their signatures. Encour-

age them to use or supply their personal or business letterhead and postage.

If you can assemble just a handful of willing volunteers to begin, that's better than none. Even if you have five willing volunteers who can each send 20 letters, that's 100 asks that might otherwise not be made.

After the letters are sent, assemble your group again to review the results and decide what's next.

When Money Is Tight, Ask Donors for Time and Ideas

Donald Hasseltine, vice president of Dickinson College (Carlisle, PA) is enjoying a fourth successful year of a five-year public campaign: He and his staff have raised more than $77 million of their $150 million goal.

Keeping in touch with donors is key to the campaign's ongoing success.

In January 2009, for example, when Hasseltine realized donor visits were down, he and his staff came up with a new engagement program — the Discovery Initiative — to connect with donors in a new way: by asking for their ideas.

Based on a similar program at Georgetown University (Washington, D.C.), the Discovery Initiative is designed to help development officers survey prospects on their feelings about Dickinson. The five-section survey (shown in part, below) features 25 questions and takes under an hour to complete.

"These are questions like you would ask in initial interviews with prospects whom you would later ask to give," Hasseltine says. "This is the same thing, only without the pressure of asking for philanthropy."

Hasseltine and his staff have made more than 200 visits this quarter — triple their visits last year, before the Discovery Initiative began. He says they have a six-month goal of 500 to 700 visits, most to major and secondary prospects, along with other members of the Dickinson community as well.

"We get to engage and grow our donor pool," Hasseltine says, "and in turn, (donors) are learning about our institution from our staff."

Additionally, Hasseltine has instituted two more programs: Dickinson 2025 and the President's Summit. Dickinson 2025 is an initiative intended to mobilize future leaders — individuals 35 to 50 years old who have taken on significant volunteer leadership and are somehow affiliated with Dickinson.

As for the President's Summit, he says: "It is common practice to invite prospects back to meet with the president. Here, we're leveraging that with the idea that the president is soliciting their advice about the strategic plan." People seem to respond well to the invitation to engage: 45 major donors are returning after last year's summit. "This approach is appealing to donors who are feeling the economic squeeze: they're able to give us something that doesn't cost money. That's good for everyone in the long run."

Source: Don Hasseltine, Vice President, Dickinson College, Dickinson College, Carlisle, PA. Phone 717-245-1029. E-mail: hasseltd@dickinson.edu

Dickinson Discovery Initiative: Survey Topics & Sample Questions

Section 1 - Attendance, experience, impact
Sample questions:
- *Tell me your Dickinson story and why you chose to attend.*
- *If you could have changed one thing about your Dickinson experience, what would it be?*

Section 2 - Current engagement
Sample questions:
- *On a scale of 1-5, how engaged with Dickinson would you consider yourself?*
- *When was the last time you visited campus?*
- *Are there services you feel Dickinson should provide to you?*

Section 3 - Perceptions of Dickinson
Sample questions:
- *In your opinion, has the college changed for the better or worse since you graduated and in what ways?*
- *In your opinion, what three schools are peers of Dickinson?*

Section 4 - Life beyond Dickinson and possible intersections with Dickinson programs
Sample questions:
- *How are you involved as an engaged citizen in your community?*
- *In what ways do you feel Dickinson prepared you to be an engaged citizen?*

Section 5 - Concluding the interview, but continuing the dialogue
Sample questions:
- *If you had to communicate one message to President Durden and the senior leadership about the school's future, your experience, an improvement to campus, what would it be?*
- *Are there other alumni whom you know who would also enjoy meeting with us?*

Build Relationships by Hosting Dinner With Seven Strangers

Try this creative approach to build relationships with donors and would-be donors alike: Invite individuals or couples to host a meal at their homes for seven persons served by your organization (e.g., students, youth, families of someone facing a specific health challenge, persons from a specific ethnic group, etc.).

What's the purpose behind the dinners? For hosts to learn more about your organization and those you serve. Hosts may discover mentoring opportunities, make lasting friendships or simply enjoy the feeling they get providing a hot, home-cooked meal for those you serve.

The dinner with seven strangers is a way to engage people in your organization that will naturally build a compelling case for support.

Donor Involvement Helps Raise Money With Little Cost

Looking for a great fundraiser that only costs time? Take the lead from Lord Fairfax Community College (LFCC) of Middletown and Warrenton, VA, where advancement staff invite donors to host and fund special events.

"Donors and friends of the college are approached to fund and host fundraising special events throughout the college's service area and invite affluent prospective donors to attend," says Linnie Carter, vice president of college advancement. "Guests are asked to make contributions to the LFCC Educational Foundation in honor of the event host."

The gifts are tax deductible and designated for a project of the host's choosing.

Usually held once a quarter with 50 to 100 guests, events typically net $20,000, says Carter. Hosts provide and fund the refreshments, venue, entertainment and costs to print and mail the invitations.

"These events are effective for the college because they expose us to a new pool of people who may not have been familiar with Lord Fairfax Community College," says Carter. "They are also effective because no expenses are incurred by the college. All money raised can immediately be put to work.

"The hosts find the events effective because they can plan a social event, invite their friends and colleagues, help a good cause and use the tax-related benefits."

Source: Linnie Carter, Vice President of College Advancement, Lord Fairfax Community College, Middletown, VA. Phone (540) 868-4077. E-mail: lcarter@lfcc.edu. Website: www.lfcc.edu

Sample Agenda for Donor-hosted Events

Tammy Haire, special events coordinator, Lord Fairfax Community College (Middletown and Warrenton, VA), says its donor-sponsored fundraisers are typically parties such as anniversaries or birthdays.

She shares a sample event agenda:

- Designated mingling period.
- Host welcomes guests and introduces college president, who speaks for a few minutes about the college and how their assistance is needed.
- A student shares his/her experience at the college.
- The host thanks everyone for attending.
- The rest of the event focuses on the party aspect.

When planning a donor-hosted event, Haire says: "Start small and start with a few trusted hosts. But most of all, encourage your hosts to have fun."

Source: Tammy Haire, Special Events Coordinator, Lord Fairfax Community College, Middletown, VA. Phone (540) 868-4076. E-mail: thaire@lfcc.edu

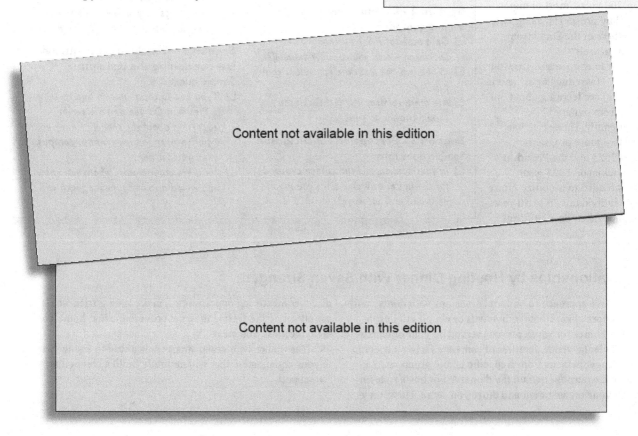

Content not available in this edition

Content not available in this edition

MORE EXAMPLES OF HOW TO INVOLVE VOLUNTEERS, BOARD MEMBERS IN FUND DEVELOPMENT

Increase Major Giving With a Targeted Subcommittee

In November 2008, volunteer fundraiser Kristy Hall took it upon herself to issue a challenge to One Home Many Hopes (OHMH), Sharon, MA, a small, start-up charity where she volunteered. Her challenge? Raise $20,000 in 30 days.

The effort would jumpstart the nonprofit, which raises money for Mudzini Kewtu, a home for abandoned and orphaned girls in Mtwapa, Kenya. Founded in November 2007, One Home Many Hopes had raised $4,000 and built a donor database of 150 in its first year.

While Hall's challenge seemed like a stretch, she actually succeeded well beyond that goal, bringing together a group of fellow volunteer fundraisers to raise $50,000 and increased One Home Many Hopes' donor database to more than 1,000 names.

One of Hall's key tricks to success was to divide her pool of fundraising volunteers into two subcommittees: one to solicit donations in the very low, $10 range, and a second subcommittee that went after much larger, $1,000 donations.

Hall recognized methods to approach the two groups would differ greatly. A major donor would want more information about where the money is going — not just to what nonprofit, but to what specific operational aspect of the nonprofit. A major donor would also want to know his/her personal values were being reflected in the nonprofit's work.

While the two subcommittees operated in some ways that were different, Hall also employed organizational methods that worked well for both of them:

❑ Forming a PR unit with additional volunteers increased media coverage, a universal approach that led to additional donations both major and minor.

❑ Scheduling a series of regular conference calls which helped to keep everyone motivated and informed of where they stood in relation to their target goals.

❑ Crafting a personal and unique pitch to donors that made OHMH stand out in the crowd among potential donors big and small.

Says John Boit, a fundraising volunteer and member of OHMH's board of directors: "We did all this in the worst economy in 80 years, with an unknown organization, in an incredibly short time frame, and at a moment when we were competing with every other organization in the world looking for year-end donations. Oh, and we didn't have a single paid person on staff — all were volunteers, working during lunch breaks and after work."

Thanks to Hall's efforts, OHMH is now a fully registered 501(c)(3) and has moved on to its next fundraising strategy: mining its donor database to encourage people to give small amounts on a recurring basis, including asking persons in the $1,000 donor level to provide the group with more financial security with smaller amounts of philanthropy.

Source: John Boit, Member, Board of Directors, One Home Many Hopes, Sharon, MA. Phone (617) 230-2574. E-mail: jboit@melwoodglobal.com

Give Class Agents Clear Expectations

All too often schools, colleges and universities will get a class agent program up and running but then fail to give agents quantifiable expectations. As a result, the program stumbles along and eventually fails.

Give your class agents a defined list of responsibilities — including deadlines — before they agree to take on the job. Here are some examples of class agent duties:

• Make a personal gift to the annual fund.

• Personally sign appeal letters directed to former classmates.

• Create and manage an e-mail forwarding list for your classmates to reconnect with one another.

• Inform your classmates of current issues and provide feedback on their interests and concerns.

• Personally thank those classmates who are supporting the institution.

• Participate in and find volunteers to help plan reunions.

• Assist in updating addresses of former classmates.

• Ask for career and personal updates from former classmates for inclusion in alumni news notes portion of [name of newsletter or magazine].

• Contact former classmates through personal visits, phone calls or correspondence between September and June to ask for their participation in your class fundraising efforts.

• Enlist former classmates as volunteers for various programs/functions.